# The Telling

The Telling

E. M. BRONER

Including The Women's Haggadah
by E.M. Broner and Naomi Nimrod

HarperSanFrancisco
A Division of HarperCollins*Publishers*

Acknowledgment to my editors:
Kandace Hawkinson, who smoothed the way.
Hilary Vartanian, who found it.

The Women's Haggadah was conceived by E. M. Broner and Naomi Nimrod
and revised by E. M. Broner in 1992.

Design and Production: Seventeenth Street Studios

L'chi Lach is from the recording, *You Shall Be a Blessing,* by Deborah Lynn
Friedman (ASCAP), Sounds Write Productions, Inc. (ASCAP) © 1989.

First Edition

Library of Congress Cataloging-in-Publication Data
Broner, E. M.
    The telling / E. M. Broner.
        p. cm.
    "Including The Women's haggadah by E. M. Broner with Naomi
Nimrod."
    Includes bibliographical references.
    1. Women in Judaism. 2. Women, Jewish—United States—Religious
life. 3. Feminism—Religious aspects—Judaism. 4. Broner, E. M. —
Religion. 5. Broner, E. M. —Friends and associates. 6. Passover—
Prayer-books and devotions—English. 7. Seder. I. Nimrod, Naomi.
II. Broner, E. M. Women's haggadah. 1993. III. Title.

    BM729.W6B75 1993
    296'.082—dc20   92–53276

    93 94 95 96 97 ❖ HAD 10 9 8 7 6 5 4 3 2 1

For
Emannuel Linden Broner
Alexandra Batya Broner
and their seders

Sari Broner and her Blessing Box
Jeremy Broner and his Wisdom

The Seder Sisters:
Phyllis Chesler
Edith Isaac-Rose
Bea Kreloff
Michele Landsberg
Letty Cottin Pogrebin
Lilly Rivlin

The Seder Mothers:
Bella Abzug
Grace Paley
Gloria Steinem

 # Contents

INTRODUCTION   *1*

PART ONE

In the Beginning

Halfway Up the Carmel, 1975   *7*
The First Seder, New York   *14*
The Second Seder, More Sisters, 1977   *24*
Mothers, Sisters, Daughters, Guests   *29*
All of Us   *39*
Spiritual Wrangling   *48*
The Symbolist   *52*

PART TWO

The Laden Table

The Laden Table   *59*

PART THREE

The Old and New Order

The Old Order   *67*
Searching for Leaven and the Four Questions   *71*
Singing the Table of Contents and the
   Blessings   *75*

PART FOUR

The Themes

The Righteous and the Veiled   *87*
Our Mothers and Our Foremothers   *97*
Grown-Up Mothers, Grown-Up Daughters   *104*

The Women and Kabbalah   *111*

Quareling and Mediating   *118*

The Strategy of Healing   *123*

Remembering   *127*

The Covenant   *130*

The Prevailing Silence   *133*

The Change Makers   *137*

PART FIVE

Community

The Ceremonies of Community   *149*

The Duties of Community   *159*

Building Community   *164*

PART SIX

Facts and Artifacts

Facts and Artifacts   *173*

Words of Mothers and Others   *184*

THE WOMEN'S HAGGADAH   *191*

Introduction

1992

RETURNING TO ISRAEL, I am located this time in the middle of Jerusalem.

I am working well.

"The air of Jerusalem makes you wise," says my neighbor, the professor.

I am feeling well.

"The air of Jerusalem makes you healthy," says my motherly neighbor, Fanny.

1975

In 1975 it was to Jerusalem that we phoned from Haifa for curious information. We, Nomi (Naomi) Nimrod and I, were working on *The Women's Haggadah* and had regendered the players. The rabbis of old became the wise women connected to them; the questions of the four sons were put into the mouths of the four daughters.

Still, we had our own questions. Since there is no neuter word in Hebrew for God, could there be a designation for holiness that was not solely male?

"Phone Jerusalem," said Nomi. "They feel closer to God there. They'll know."

By "they," Nomi meant the first women rabbinical students who were doing their year abroad at Hebrew Union College.

"What do you call You Know Who?" we asked, once we got the crackly line to Jerusalem.

"Shekhinah," they answered, "She Who Dwells in Our Midst."

"Oh, yes!" we said.

The Shekhinah is a Kabbalistic concept, the female aspect of God. She is addressed in prayer, especially during the holidays of Sukkoth and the arrival of the New Moon. The sage

Rabbi Yonahan, said, "Whoever blesses the New Moon at the proper time is considered as having welcomed the presence of the Shekhinah."

Etymologically, *Shikoon* is neighborhood. *Shekena* is a neighbor. We could nicely use such a neighborly presence as She Who Dwells in Our Midst.

It is said in Israel, "One works in Haifa, plays in Tel Aviv, and prays in Jerusalem." We tried then, in 1975, to work and pray and play in Haifa. We worked at writing a new kind of prayer, using the spine of the traditional holidays, to put women between the covers of the Haggadah, the traditional booklet used at Passover to recount the Exodus. We played with new ideas and we rested, Nomi and I. But even at rest we were uncomfortable with the information we were excavating about the extent of the ancient misogyny.

We were uncomfortable with each decision: What to retain and what to restate? How to keep bitterness and anger from overwhelming us? Where to place the traditional stories and yet insert new characters?

I think when we first wrote, "We were slaves unto Pharaoh and the Shekhinah brought us forth," we felt we had invoked the name that would instill strength into us.

And when we said, "We recline on this night for the unhurried telling of the legacy of Miriam," we had our main character who would encapsulate our journey.

Miriam was the sister of Moses and Aaron. She was the first prophet and she foretold the Exodus; she was the singer at the seashore and the one cast low. After her outcry, "Has the Lord spoken only through Moses?" she was publicly humiliated. Soon thereafter, she died. Nothing more. Only five times was she mentioned in early Hebrew scripture—once in Exodus and four times in Numbers. Yet she has haunted our prophets and tellers of legend.

For instance, the prophet Micah speaks with God's voice: "For I brought thee up out of the land of Egypt, / and redeemed thee out of the house of bondage; / and I sent before thee Moses, Aaron, and Miriam." (Micah 6).

And, among the many legends dealing with Miriam, in contrast to the narrow space she occupies in early scripture, is the one of Miriam and the well. In Miriam's honor, a well of clear, cool water followed the children of Israel through the desert. When Miriam died, the well dried up and disappeared.

We were that well of longing for our history, that well of words pouring forth.

Although Miriam is the parentheses of Exodus, beginning it by peering at the baby, ending it singing at the shore of the Reed Sea, she is a structure, a construct. What had been omitted from her history was also omitted from our mythic past. It was clearly time for a new Telling.

Nomi and I resolved that we, her modern daughters, would sing Miriam's songs, would reconstruct her journey, and build upon it our own journeys.

Nomi and I parted early in the winter of 1976, shortly after the year began, as we were doing rewrites on our Haggadah. We reunited once or twice briefly, at conferences. We went our separate ways. Nomi moved to a kibbutz with her lover, Haggai, taught there, and bore four daughters. I went through the desert, each year retelling the story, carrying our combined effort, *The Women's Haggadah*.

## PART ONE

In the Beginning

Halfway Up the Carmel, 1975

WITH WOMEN, holiday begins before ceremony, with cleaning, preparation, presentation. If seder is order, that Spring of '75 we changed the order.

Perhaps it was living near HaNavi, the Street of the Prophet, in Haifa, or going up the mountain to teach at the University of Haifa. Or having that Olympic view of the harbor far below. Or the valley beneath our balcony, stretching before us to the sea.

The streets where we, my husband Robert and I, lived during our academic leaves and sabbaticals in Israel always seemed prophetic. In 1972 we lived in Jerusalem on HaMagid, the Street of the Storyteller. There I wrote stories and began to gather the material for a novel to be called *A Weave of Women*.

In Haifa in 1975 our cross streets were the Street of Leonardo da Vinci—appropriate for Bob, an artist—and the Street of the Prophet Elijah. In the tradition of prophets, Elijah lived in a cave in the Carmel Mountains, thinking his deep and dark thoughts. Indeed, it is the song to Elijah which we sing every Passover that may have turned my thoughts so often in '75 to Exodus.

Mysticism was in the air. Perhaps that's why we, three women—a Member of Parliament, a social worker, and I—announced somewhat hubristically that we were holding a "Seder of the North."

But this would be different. The invited men would prepare the meal, serve, and clean. The women would contemplate the traditional Haggadah and write new and relevant prayers.

The American men agreed. Bob made a potato kugel. Michael and Davida Cohen drove in from their *moshav*, a cooperative farm, Michael bearing his lemon-stuffed chicken breasts while Davida thought of additions to the Haggadah.

Michael had been the owner of a restaurant, Spinoza's Blintzes, in Berkeley, California, during the sixties. During the student antiwar activism, the Berkeley police gassed the campus and the restaurant, a popular hangout. The odor of gas lingered until Michael decided to leave the country.

"I cannot live in a state where Reagan is governor," he said.

When he and Davida left the *moshav* and returned to the States, they lived in a country where Reagan was president.

Marcia Freedman, American-born member of the Israeli Knesset, or parliament, came with women's prayers. Nomi Nimrod, social worker, composed a prayer of Miriam driven mad by losing her role as prophet. I wrote the questions of the four daughters instead of the traditional questions of the four sons. Bob and I both sat at the head of the table, each wearing a yarmulke, friends and neighbors surrounding us.

Some of the Israelis resisted this role change, certainly our neighbors. The father and son kept to their chairs during the cooking, serving, cleaning up. The woman of the family bawled out an invited singer with, "What will you be when you grow older without a man? Your voice will go and then you'll be nothing." The woman singer stopped singing.

In spite of these interruptions something so startling had happened in that sweet clementine season, something so different emerged from our apartment with its terrazzo floors, that we could actually hear the difference out the window. At the base of the mountain, in the middle, or at the top people were reading and singing the Passover service. But our songs had different lyrics.

The next morning Nomi Nimrod phoned. We agreed to meet to talk about delving into sources and writing our own service.

The idea both excited and shocked us.

And so we met daily, despite my teaching and her working schedules, despite the demands of our families.

When we began reading and writing in the study of her late father, a learned cantor, we expected thunder and lightning to come through the roof and crack the walls of the library.

The mother of my collaborator peered anxiously at us

from the doorway. What were we doing in her husband's study? Were we desecrating what he had consecrated? His death was so recent that his books were not yet dusty as we pored over them. His widow was sure we were going out of our depth, neither of us Judaic scholars.

Nomi Nimrod and I *were* out of our depth, for our lives interfered with our contemplative time.

Rivke, Nomi's mother, tapped at the study door. She was Orthodox, trained to serve and, disapproving though she was, nevertheless she carried in tea and biscuits.

We had other kinds of rappings at our study time. With women, the world is never left outside. Nomi worried that she would lose her job as a social worker among disadvantaged girls. There was already talk in the office. Some said she was setting a bad example, being pregnant without marriage.

Nomi's mother had heart trouble, and her heart was troubled the more by Nomi's pregnancy. Nomi held the founding kibbutz theory about marriage as an exploitative, capitalistic institution. She and her kibbutznik lover, Haggai, made their separate lives, he in a kibbutz in the Jezreel Valley and she doing social work in Haifa.

I had daughters in Israel and sons in the States. My youngest daughter, Nahama, was with us, doing her high school by correspondence that semester. Her older sister, Sari, was living in Kfar Blum, a kibbutz on the Lebanese border. Sari was a volunteer in the greenhouse, working in the rose garden. She told of the anthropomorphic tree toads with long prehensile fingers clinging to the rosebush stems and staring directly at her. She spoke of the fawn nibbling at the grass around the kibbutz Olympic-size swimming pool. Sari had spent three years traveling and wondered if the kibbutz was her destination or just another stop along the way.

My sons, Adam and Jeremy, were at MIT that year. How were they doing at a highly competitive university, without regular contact with us?

There was another distraction, this one in the cantor's study, a large, full-length mirror. Nomi regarded her burgeoning belly during our mornings of work. She tossed her long brown hair, watched her full lips move as she talked.

One day she turned the mirror away from her. She was a beauty and decided the time in the study was not for vanity.

Nomi and I were on sanctified ground, reading orthodox text, two women unorthodox in their lives and their approach to the subject.

As always, when Nomi and I worked, we spread the books before us at the great library table. Rivke silently watched Nomi ripening. Rivke and Nomi had not been speaking, though they shared the house. But something happened to make them talk.

Bob was teaching painting and silk screen in the Art and Art History Department, and I was teaching a course in the English Department that began as Contemporary Literature and ended up as Women's Studies. It was the first such taught at Haifa university or, indeed, at any Israeli university. Nomi was auditing the course.

I had assigned the class Doris Lessing's *The Summer Before the Dark,* about a woman's aging and her discovery of invisibility as she grayed and lost her supple figure.

"Is it really a dark period to be feared?" I asked the class. "Invite your mothers and we will ask them. They are the experts."

Nomi broke her silence and invited her mother to class. The daughters questioned their mothers. In the course of the discussion on aging, Rivke and Nomi at last turned to each other and talked.

"Children are like bad pennies," said Rivke during that class. "They turn up until the end of your days." Nomi blinked at this. But both mother and daughter stayed on auditing the class, doing their assignments together.

Rivke never interrupted our writing sessions, but she began to sit with us daily and knit in the study. She heard our shock over the extent of the misogyny that we were uncovering. The difficulty for us was to be able to emerge once we had immersed ourselves in it. And Rivke feared for us.

"Better to burn the words of the Torah than to let women read them," Nomi quoted an ancient sage, Rabbi Eliezer ben Hyrcannus, to his wife, Ima Shalom. We discovered that Ima Shalom was the daughter of a rabbi, the granddaughter of a rabbi, and herself learned. We would get even with old Hyrcannus, we resolved.

All we could do was turn our hurt and anger into our work. *The Women's Haggadah* became a product of that feeling of both excitement and betrayal. The excitement lay in discovering the scholarly women connected to the sages of old, even to some of the rabbis mentioned in the traditional Haggadah. Among the rabbis "sitting all through the night, telling Israel's story . . . singing the songs at the Passover table" were "Eliezer the great and Rabbi Akiva the bold."

The women who lit up our studies were: Rachel, wife of Rabbi Akiva; Beruriah, wife of Rabbi Meir; Ima Shalom, wife of Rabbi Eliezer ben Hyrcannus; and Ima Shalom's niece, unnamed, daughter of Rabbi Gamliel. If we had been betrayed, known only by connection to famous men, then we would avenge ourselves by revealing, by enlarging our matrilineage.

One day Rivke lifted her head from her knitting and spoke.

"A friend and I once went to visit Martin Buber," she said. "We, too, were searching in the Torah. Buber shook his finger at us. 'If you delve too deeply, you will discover dangerous things.'

"I took his advice," said Rivke, "and stopped looking."

During one writing session, Rivke heard us exclaiming.

"What is it?" she asked, alarmed.

"There are almost no women mentioned in that first Exodus of Abraham and Sarah."

Rivke stood up. She put on her *kova,* the Israeli cloth cap, against the strong midday sun. She took her purse by the handles, collected a notepad, and informed us, "I will find the women."

In the heat of the noon sun she took the long bus ride from the center of the mountain to its base where the Maritime Museum rests.

"Surely," Rivke thought, "with all the ancient artifacts, all those representations of the sea with people crossing, women will be represented. How is it not possible?"

Rivke asked to see the museum's extensive collection of woodcuts, coins, artifacts based on the movements of people. It was not possible, but no women were depicted leaving Egypt.

"How could there be a Jewish people if there were no women?" Rivke asked the curator in exasperation.

She did not even have to dig deeply, as Buber had warned, to discover that she had no history.

At last she understood our struggles.

Rivke herself could not struggle much longer. That trip in the hot sun exhausted her. She, frail since the death of her husband, seemed to take up less and less room in the house.

During one writing session she had a heart attack. I remember clutching my notes and following the stretcher into the hospital alongside Nomi, while Rivke scolded me, "Go home and work, Essie. Go to work!"

Rivke recovered that time. Nomi and I finished the first draft of our Haggadah.

It was the end of June 1975. Time to pack, to leave my students, the sight of Haifa rising out of the sea, and the hilly surroundings that the proud residents called "Little Switzerland." My daughters returned with us to continue their education. My sons were safe in Cambridge.

Soon after my return to the States I received a letter or cablegram, I cannot remember which now: "I am an orphan. Come to me. Nomi."

I wrote back immediately, "I will win a large award. Then I will be able to come to you."

How do we know these things before they happen? I had written a play while I was in Haifa and mailed it to the American Bicentennial Playwriting Contest. I won the first prize of three thousand dollars plus a full production.

I bought fare to Haifa, to Nomi and her baby, Ruth, in December of '75.

"I have to take you someplace," said Nomi.

She wrapped Ruth against the wind, and we drove down to the sea near the Maritime Museum where Rivke was buried.

◆　◆　◆　◆

It was four months later, Spring of '76, when two groups of women gathered, one on West End Avenue in Manhattan, the other on Derech HaYam, Path of the Sea, in Haifa. Both groups had the same text, one in Hebrew, the other in English. Both groups were doing something simple but radical, declaring their right to holiday.

Marcia Freedman, Knesset member then, described what happened in Haifa in her memoir, *Exile in the Promised Land* (Ithaca, NY: Firebrand Press, 1990):

> At *Pesach* forty women gathered to celebrate an alternative *seder,* the ritual meal. For the occasion Nomi Nimrod [coauthor of the text] and I moved the furniture out of the living room and covered the floor with cushions and mattresses. We placed dozens of candles all around the room. The women brought food: hummus, t'china, tabouleh, koobeh, pita bread. We reclined on the mattresses, leaned on pillows, were bathed in soft candlelight and read together from the Haggadah that Nomi and Esther Broner had just finished writing. Nomi led us, wearing her dead father's cantorial robes. We spoke of the few women mentioned in the Talmud— Bruriah, Ima Shalom, Rachel the wife of Akiva, and lastly the unnamed daughter of Rabbi Gamliel. We spoke of Miriam the prophetess, and we spoke of ourselves, the oppression of the Jews in exile flowing naturally into the oppression of women in Israel. We talked through the night and into the morning, dozing off now and then on the floor. The *seder* lasted until the next day. (p. 130.)

In the morning, Jenny Freedman, Marcia's young daugh-ter, rose to find the women stretched out on the carpets, on chairs, lying on the couch. Jenny informed them that it was morning.

It is said in the traditional Haggadah that in the morning the rabbis were informed that the cock had crowed and it was time to say the morning prayers.

The congregation of women who had spent the night in deep discussion, eating of the fruits and nuts of the earth, and had dozed languidly on the Arabic rugs, now left the apart-ment on Derech HaYam to go on with their lives.

In New York, the group we were forming did much the same thing.

The First Seder, New York

WHEN WE THINK about the first seder in New York in 1976, those of us who were there were altered.

"I feel," said Letty Cottin Pogrebin, "when I think about the seder, a spiritual nucleus for the whole year, a certain kind of transcendence. When there is the seder, it is satisfying and magical."

"I discovered," said Gloria Steinem, "for the first time the purpose of ritual, to make an open space, or a path, for emotions to happen. I thought it was wonderful. Those of us who were motherless became each other's mothers. I have been in my life more refugee than community."

"As far as a community of the seder was concerned," said Letty, "I was happy that smart Jewish feminists were willing to be publicly smart Jewish feminists. There was an organic Judaism increased by a feminist incarnation."

From then on we were a tribe. We were a group of women who met once in innocence, achieved a spiritual bonding, and stubbornly continued meeting, planning, and quarreling.

If that is community—"It is not!" Letty assured me—or if it is family—"Chosen family," said Gloria—it has been more than an ongoing novelty and, therefore, demands the Telling of it.

I am not the only one to tell. There could be as many tales as there are Seder Sisters. However, I entered this history before it was historic.

The year 1976 *was* historic, a year of literary outpouring in the women's movement, fiction, essay, psychology, and art history. Many of the books would become classics. Among the literary works were Marge Piercy's *Woman on the Edge of Time,* Margaret Atwood's *Surfacing,* Maxine Hong Kingston's *The Woman Warrior,* Alice Walker's *Meridian.* Feminist literary criticism saw the release of *Literary Women, The Great Writers* by Ellen Moers. In theology, sociology, psychology, and sexuality, there were Merlin Stone's *When God Was a Woman,* Adrienne Rich's *Of Woman Born,* Dorothy Dinnerstein's *The Mermaid and the Minotaur,* and Shere Hite's *The Hite Report.* All of these titles were sandwiched between the 1975 release of Susan Brownmiller's landmark *Against Our Will: Men, Women and Rape,* and *The Women's Room,* the 1977 best-seller by Marilyn French. Feminist writers were on a roll.

As for artists, there were more one-woman art shows in 1976 than ever before (and perhaps since). It was also the year when the traveling exhibition *Women Artists: 1550–1950* came to the Brooklyn Museum, curated and cataloged by Ann Sutherland Harris and Linda Nochlin.

The air was stirring.

It was also the year of feminist religious awakening. The Episcopalian women gave themselves the right to perform that which their church had denied them, ordination for the priesthood.

In 1976, two young undergraduate religion majors, Naomi Janowitz and Maggie Wenig, brought out the *Brown College Siddur Nashim,* a Sabbath prayer book in which, on the first day of menstruation, God is thanked for the covenant of blood with women.

> Lord our God and God of our mothers, accept this day my offering of blood.
> It is a sign between You and Your daughters. . . . For You not only created us but breathed into us the breath of life, which is blood and You renew, every month, that life within us.
> That blood is a gift from You to us. . . .

Nineteen seventy-six was the year of the First Feminist Seder, when four of us who would became regular participants gathered: Phyllis Chesler, Letty Cottin Pogrebin, Gloria Steinem, and I. And we had other guests as well.

At our initial meeting in New York, our differences were apparent. Gradually, our similarities became evident.

Two came from *Ms.* magazine, both blond, lithe, with glasses and long, straight hair—Gloria Steinem and Letty

Cottin Pogrebin. Phyllis Chesler was a dark, voluptuous contrast.

Chesler and I had met in 1975, the year before, when she had come to Haifa University to speak. After her talk we went to the apartment Bob and I rented in the *merkaz,* the center of town. There Nomi and I showed her *The Women's Haggadah,* which we were just completing. Chesler was much taken with it.

Chesler was an enthusiast. She spoke about a play she had seen at BAM, the Brooklyn Academy of Music, Leah Napolin's adaptation of I. B. Singer's story, *Yentl.*

"The play is spiritual! It's feminist!" exulted Chesler. "We have to get it moved from BAM to Broadway! It has to be seen by everybody."

Eventually, it was.

Chesler charged in when there were good feminist deeds to be done.

"We'll put on *The Women's Haggadah!*" she said.

And she did, not on Broadway but West End Avenue.

◆ ◆ ◆ ◆

The women crowded the foyer, looking suspiciously into the living room. There the Oriental rug had been rolled against the wall, and a tablecloth covered the floor, spread with candlesticks, matzoth, and a seder plate with the symbols of the holiday. My coauthored *Women's Haggadah,* xeroxed by Chesler, was piled in a corner. Pillows surrounded the tablecloth invitingly.

Still the women tarried.

"Let us get started," I said.

No one stirred.

I was the stranger in the strange land. I was from the Midwest and an academician. Though I had published both academic and literary works, I was not a New York writer. I was an unknown to these women. And New Yorkers are not friendly to the unknown.

Then I realized that a beginning requires a dramatic gesture, a change of costume. I reached up my hands and pinned on my yarmulke.

"Daughters," I said, "it's time to light the candles."

These were my contemporaries. Why did I say, "Daughters"? Perhaps I was declaring myself their *rebbe,* teacher.

The women obediently followed me into the living room, each standing by a pillow. At my pillow was my Haggadah with its notes, emendations, additional verses, as well as the order of procedure. I had set up my little corner of artifacts, including a book of matches. I stood with the other women and lit the candles. This was *Shabbat Gadol,* the time where Sabbath and another holiday—in this case, Passover—combine.

The women stared. Their *bubehs,* their grandmothers, may have done this. Certainly not most of their mothers. I covered my eyes and made three circles, enlarging from self to family to community. When I prayed in the feminine to the Shekhinah, those who knew Hebrew blinked in surprise. Then the women seated themselves on the floor.

Andrea Dworkin was there, curly haired, hefty, wearing her traditional garb of overalls and perspiring in the closeness of the seating. She would bring out book after book on battered women, on women of the New Right, on pornography. Next to her, plump and talkative, was Aviva Cantor Zuckoff, the bringer of the *shomrei* matzo, round and specially baked. Aviva was formerly of *Hadassah* magazine, from which she had just been fired for being too feminist. In response, she cofounded *Lilith,* the Jewish feminist magazine.

Miss USA, Summer Bartholomew, looked unlike the rest of us with her heavy makeup, coiffed hair, and sexy clothes at a time when we were giddy with the freedom of loose-fitting garments. I remember her being shy and hesitant, and I wondered why Chesler had invited her after a chance meeting on an airplane. The reason became apparent when Summer told her tale of beauty betrayed, of the pageants making a profit on women and the women left with little for their efforts.

There was a lesbian couple, a dusky-skinned Lebanese woman and her pale companion. This closeted couple insisted that we listen, and we stayed up most of the night hearing not only the revisionist Haggadah but other tellings, such as what it was like to be undercover, separated from society as the women couple related it.

I blessed the daughters of the seder. On Shabbat night, it is traditional for the "head of the house," the father, to bless the children. I wanted these women to know that blessings came from connection, not gender or age.

With great nervousness—for I was a novice at this—I assumed an elegiac voice.

I spoke of the seder with its "rites and wrongs / forgettings and longings / *morror* and *matok* / the bitter and the sweet." I said I was their "scribe / inscribing their pain." I was their "memory and ancestry."

By candlelight, as I proclaimed myself their voice, I heard a collective sigh. No one had spoken for them in such a manner. There were thirteen of us, like the number of months of the Hebrew calendar, like the number of times a woman bleeds in a year.

I asked that we introduce ourselves by our matrilineage. No one had made such a request of them before.

"I am Esther," I began, "Daughter of Bronya, granddaughter of Nechama and Tsivia. That is as far back as I know. Who were your mothers?"

Some listed their biological mothers, others their teachers or mentors.

Martha Graham was the mentor for Joan Anker, trained as a dancer.

We drew courage from the example of strong women and they became our "mothers." In 1976 many of our mothers looked askance at these hubristic daughters who were searching a new way.

"I was my own mother," said Gloria Steinem.

GLORIA

Gloria's voice was Midwestern like mine. She once said, "If Esther and I could make it out of Detroit and Toledo, then anyone can."

She did not speak to attack, to personalize in anger. She blamed no one, not even her mother, who could not mother her.

I would learn that her background was checkered—living in a trailer or in a house about to tumble down. Her father was Jewish, her mother Christian. Her mother, Ruth, had been a journalist. After marriage, she became a "dutiful," homebound wife, while the husband, a salesman, went frequently on the road. The father both nurtured Gloria and left her in charge of her depressed mother and the daily fare. The mother and daughter lived marginally.

At one point during those young years, Gloria became interested in Christian fundamentalism, taking a bus across town to church. There had to be an alternative world, a life better than the one in the cramped trailer or the drafty house. Still, obedience was too great a price to pay for belief.

So she mothered herself. But Ruth Steinem, drifting in and out of her depressions, incapacitated in her daily life, managed to sell the tumbledown house and raise the money for her daughter's college tuition to Smith. And then Gloria was awarded a Fulbright scholarship to India.

Gloria, of the Christian first name and Jewish last name, would become a mother of the seder. And *mother* would be a word from holy to intimate in her seder vocabulary.

At one seder Gloria would say, "We are trying to unite the great cosmic mother," that deity, once the earth mother, then torn asunder. "It is that spirit of earth, of nature, a cosmic union that we have lost," mourned Gloria.

Her loss was personal and universal.

PHYLLIS
As Gloria spoke, Phyllis Chesler perhaps was thinking about her mother and mothering.

As Gloria was raised in blue-collar Toledo, Phyllis was born and raised in Brooklyn to a deliveryman father and an Orthodox mother. The mother was restrained in display of affection to her daughter, and the father easily exercised by his daughter's exuberance.

How frightening for a traditional mother to have birthed a brilliant and demanding daughter, even moreso than the favored sons! How worrisome for the father to have a young daughter with a prematurely developing body! She must have done something wrong to have become womanly so soon.

Also, Phyllis loved learning—in English, in Hebrew.

"Hebrew?" said her mother. "What do you need yeshiva for? A girl doesn't need learning."

When Phyllis was finishing her doctorate in psychology, she also decided to go to medical school. She finished a year or two.

"Medical school?" she was asked. "What does a girl need medical school for?"

She may have dropped out of yeshiva and medical school, but she applied herself to feminist studies of women and mental institutions, women and custody of their children, women and surrogate motherhood.

She may have been her own mother also.

"Who is your mother?" The question echoed in the room.

LETTY

Letty's mother had died when Letty was a young girl. Letty has spoken and written since in her memoir, *Deborah, Golda, and Me* (New York: Crown, 1991), of how her mother had "kitchen religion," a mixture of daily love and superstition—holidays lovingly prepared, yet—moonlight on the bed? Pooh pooh, spit over your shoulder, and pull down the shade.

Letty was a smiler. She had entered the living room interestedly. Her background differed from that of Gloria or Phyllis in being one of propriety and privilege. Only later did we learn that with her mother's death Letty was unhoused from family and religion. She was not allowed by her father to mourn her mother formally, though Letty's father had insisted that she have formal religious education. When her father remarried, she found her belongings stacked against a wall. She slept on a cot in her former home, her mother's silver Sabbath candlesticks lit by the new wife.

◆　◆　◆　◆

If these women had been novelists instead of memoirists, perhaps the data would have been too difficult to read, the dust covers removed from the internal furniture. And all would be crying, "Mama! Mama! Why have your forsaken me?"

◆　◆　◆　◆

I asked the gathered women at the First Feminist Seder about their own plagues:

Interruptiveness
Lack of Honor
Lack of Quiet
Lack of Self

The plague for the women couple was clearly ostracism. We all sank deeper and deeper on to our elbows as the evening wore on, listening to the story of their love. In 1976 some of us had not heard this information, and the women's movement had not taken it in either. Perhaps this passionate discourse with women of the press this night would help change perceptions.

When we came to the traditional part in the Haggadah of the Promises God Kept, *V'he Shamda,* I spoke about the Promises Not Kept, *V'He ShLo Amda:*

Daughters, tell of the promises broken.
The promise of eternal beauty
The promise of eternal love
The promise of eternal health
The promise of stability
The promise of the dream
All these and more broken

The promise of dignity
The promise of peace
The promise of war and victory
All promises not kept

The promise of the past
The promise of the future
All, all promises broken.

The promise of childhood
The promise of maturity
The dignity of age
broken

The promise of closeness
The promise of privacy and distance
broken.

"I was promised that if I was a good girl," said Aviva Cantor, "and went to school and made good grades, I would be rewarded. I was a good girl. I studied hard. I made those good grades. I was well educated. But the promise was broken. No honor, no respect was accorded me."

The former dancer Joan Anker felt that after training and forming a dance company, there was the promise of a career. But in an auto accident on tour, her back was broken, as was that particular career. She was promised time as her children grew, but her time was always interrupted.

◆　◆　◆　◆

It was well past midnight when we opened the door and welcomed Mother Miriam. It was the first time we had done such a thing. It was also the first time that we spoke in ritual of our mothers, of our stolen legacy, and of our spiritual longings.

Four of us would became regular sedergoers and establish the ritual of the Telling: talking of our past in a new way, talking of ourselves openly and confidentially, connecting ourselves to legend, and, thereby, becoming legendary.

Although we were feminists, we had much to separate, to divide us—our personalities, backgrounds, geographic locale even, our visibility out in the world. I was newly visible to these women.

ESTHER

I learned that first night that, contrary to my rearing, I could lead a group, invent ritual, even be scholarly in a subject then not easily accessible to women.

The world of academia was opening to women. Many of us who had been instructors were climbing up the ladder to where the air was more rarefied, where only a few women were becoming professors. Because of the effect of Ellen Moers's *Literary Women: The Great Writers,* I would have my first doctoral student whose dissertation would be a new way of viewing literature, informed by women's studies.

But the world of sacred space was not women's space.

The men of my family are Men of Worth, my father, my brothers. But that phrase, when applied to women, has an altered meaning. Every Friday night my father read, from Proverbs, *Eshet Hayal,* Woman of Worth, to my mother, kissing her sweetly afterward. The man was at the gates of the city, speaking of matters of state, while the province of the woman was her household.

At Chesler's I was standing at the gates of the city. I had invaded the territory of the men of my family. That I had not done before.

And I worried. How would this curious document, which regendered our customary holiday, play?

Gloria was startled. It was her first ritual. It was feminist, poetic, participatory. There was room in the women's movement for the spiritual.

Letty was shocked. She has said that it brought her back to Judaism, combining feminism and ceremony with tradition.

And Phyllis was very proud. She had staged a successful event. She had chosen the guests and opened her house to them. She was a spiritual impressario.

The Second Seder, More Sisters, 1977

WE WERE ALL so high in 1976, it did not seem possible to come down in '77.

In 1977 *Ms.* magazine, under Letty's careful editing, excerpted *The Women's Haggadah*. Phyllis's name was omitted as the one who publicly presented the seder. Although *Ms.* apologized and acknowledged her role the next month, from then on Phyllis viewed the event with apprehension and suspicion. Honor could so easily be taken away. One always had to be prepared to fight for it.

We had sporadic contacts with one another during the year, I still teaching in Detroit at Wayne State University and, on the phone, editing the *Haggadah* with Letty. I would hear Phyllis's hurt voice also over the phone.

Gloria and Letty urged that we again hold a woman's seder. Phyllis had some hesitation about attending but, when she arrived, she brought friends who remain with us to this day.

We held the seder in the new loft that Bob and I bought—for a song—in New York, four thousand square feet with no partitions, the elevator opening on to the floor, three pull-string toilets against the wall, whose high cabinets filled and sprinkled those who sat below.

We had no furniture but did have the requisite pillows for reclining on Passover for the Telling of the Tale. The walls of the loft, a former sewing machine factory, had been painted white, and the floors were newly sanded, polyurethaned, and treacherously slippery. Our voices echoed as if we were in a hall.

"The daughters came and we all sat around on cushions," Gloria remembers. "The first and second seders were revelatory, warm, lyrical, mythic."

Letty's eleven-year-old daughters came, Abigail and Robin. An artist, Phoebe Helman, brought her daughter,

Maya Sonenberg, about fifteen then. Nahama, my sixteen-year-old daughter, was there as a guide while the children searched for *hametz,* leftover bread crumbs, the detritus of the past year. With feather and candle they brushed windowsills, behind radiators, on all the ledges, looking for the crumbs of the past year. The loft was dark, scary, only lit by a lamp or two, and the girls were hesitant, wide-eyed, holding the feather out before them on their search.

We could scarcely know that in a decade or more the daughters would lead the mothers.

The seder was written up in various newspapers. Gloria Steinem was quoted in a Baltimore paper speaking excitedly of her first spiritual event. Women around the country were shown the *Ms.* version of *The Women's Haggadah* by their daughters. In Toronto, Michele Landsberg cut the excerpted version out of the magazine and used it at her family seder.

Among us, we were forming a community: Letty, Phyllis, Gloria, I, and the newcomers, Bea and Lilly, as well as our daughters and, soon, surrogate daughters.

I never referred to the sedergoers as "daughters" again, for we were all growing up together.

LILLY

Lilly was tall, shapely, with long hair curling around her youthful face and a camera slung over her shoulder. This splendidly dressed person focused her camera on the young daughters we invited to this seder. Lilly, on her heels, slid across the slippery floor following her subjects. Some of those earliest atmospheric pictures were taken by Lilly, the children hunting for leaven with feather and candle, their faces candlelit.

Lilly Rivlin is a fifth-generation Jerusalemite, displaced to the States. Her family is famous for politicians, religious leaders, scribes, and one Tel Aviv art dealer who proclaimed his independence by changing his name.

Lilly depicted a gathering of the Rivlin family in her first film, *The Tribe,* five thousand strong meeting in Jerusalem from all over the world. In the film, Lilly, as narrator, says that she is the black sheep of the family. That family, which seemed to be about continuity and accomplishment, did not have place for a freelancer, a free spirit like Lilly.

Like the scribes, the historians in the Rivlin family, Lilly became our documenter, filming a documentary of our Ninth Seder. Her film, *Miriam's Daughters Now,* has been shown on National Public Television as well as at many film festivals.

Like most of us, Lilly Rivlin came from working-class parents in Washington, D.C. Her father owned a bar. Her mother was a passive woman. Neither was supportive of this beautiful and ambitious daughter, who always had to make her own way. She received a Defense Department scholarship in the sixties to work on her doctorate (as did many students). At UC Berkeley, she studied neutralism in Asia. Called "the Israeli" by the other students, she would stride tall across the campus, her long, wavy, black hair flying. It was natural that she would be active in the Berkeley Free Speech Movement.

"Why do you need a doctorate?" asked her graduate professor. "Marry me and you'll have one by proxy."

She did and, as one must with proxy husbands, ultimately shed him. Lilly is always on the edge, the risky edge, as is the world of the freelancer. In a way, she is the freest of us, always attempting to bridge opposing forces: Palestinian/ Israeli; African-American/Jewish.

As the depression of the eighties came down on us, Lilly suffered. She would work harder; there were fewer jobs in the public or private section, never mind fund-raising for one's own films. She is her own support, her own comfort.

On several seders Lilly has spoken or delivered *midrashim* on the prophet Miriam.

"Those of us who are single women have Miriam as a role model," she has told us during the seders. "She was a care-taker, an enabler."

These attributes are also Lilly's.

BEA

Another member of the community from the Second Seder on is Bea Kreloff.

"Phyllis brought us all together," Bea reminds me.

Bea is Russian-looking with large, almond-shaped eyes. She could have been camp counselor, group mother, almost the stereotypical Jewish mother, fussing and concerned about each of us, feeding us, visiting us in times of our need. The only thing that made her choose another life was that she was, in her soul, an artist, and, in her body, a woman who loves women. She is one of those women who follow a path, marry for twenty-four years, bear children, then suddenly veer off to create themselves. Helen Yglesias wrote about Bea using a pseudonym for her in the nonfiction book *Starting Early, Anew, Over, and Late* (New York: Rawson, Wade, 1978); the book is about women who, in their middle years, change their lives.

Bea was raised in Brighton Beach, her father a clothing designer. Not long ago there was the premier of a documentary, *Brighton Beach*. We gave a loft party for the showing, everyone coming with TV sets of every size, from hand-held to portable carried in with difficulty. From each set emerged Bea's voice telling about her babyhood in Brighton Beach. She spoke of her parents swimming out in the water every morning, even during the cold weather, while they set this chubby baby on the sand to dig. She would see them swimming facing each another, talking over the day to come, turning and coming back the same way, the day decided. The sun would make a gleaming path on the water while the baby filled her pail.

Bea was trained to believe you could be everything and anything. She belonged to each group in her area, from *Heder,* Hebrew school, to the Young Communist League. She chose Washington Irving High School in Manhattan, traveling on the subway from Brooklyn. There, even as a youngster, she took life drawing classes. In English class she worked on the school literary magazine, her English teacher an elegant lady who lived on Gramercy Park, inviting her class to tea weekly. The students went to concert halls. It was a school for the training of cultured people, though they came from every class and every part of the city. Bea married early. There were not many options open in those days for girls from traditional families. Soon after, her mother died, scarcely in her fifties.

"Each day I live past fifty is a gift," says Bea. "But I miss my mother every one of those days."

Bea and her husband had just moved away from Brooklyn, into a Manhattan apartment. When her mother died, Bea, ever the dutiful daughter, returned home with her husband to housekeep for her father, disturbed brother, and younger sister.

"No one ever told me I didn't have to," said Bea. "I had no one to talk to. My father was prosperous. He could have afforded a housekeeper."

Bea postponed her life for twenty years. She took art classes at the Brooklyn Museum, painting while her babies slept in their strollers in her studio. She raised her sons and was active in integrating the community schools. She took women lovers. And finally she took the reins into her own hands, left Brooklyn for Westbeth, the artists' housing project.

When we met, that Second Seder in 1977, Bea, without formal degrees, was made head of the Art Department at the Ethical Culture Fieldston School. She had picked up her brushes, becoming the bohemian she had dreamed of being, probably since she saw her parents swimming out to sea and back again.

Bea Kreloff brought to our community warmth, *mamaloshen,* the mother tongue, and a commitment to the politics of her community and to peace.

Bea fiercely keeps us informed and active. She is committed to the lesbian community, grieves with those young men stricken with and dying of AIDS. She urges us into action when we become complacent. She is our own seder whip, and, when not whipping, she loves us.

After the Second Feminist Seder in 1977, the seders became more sophisticated, perhaps less spontaneous and intimate, with specific themes, parts given out to the participants, discussion over the guest list, and the assignment of what to bring to the table.

Mothers, Sisters, Daughters, Guests

AT FIRST we were the Seder Makers. Then there seemed to be tiers: the worker bees, eventually seven of us who did the pre-seder planning and meetings; then three who were inspirational to us but who, we felt, did not have the time for the drudge work: Gloria Steinem, Bella Abzug, and Grace Paley. Lastly, there was the changing array of guests.

The planners were eventually Bea Kreloff, Edith Isaac-Rose, Michele Landsberg, Phyllis Chesler, Letty Pogrebin, Lilly Rivlin, and I, and we called ourselves the Seder Sisters. Those who inspired us we called the Seder Mothers.

From the Second Seder, 1977, on, we invited our daughters. They did not always accept our invitations. Their own lives were of primary importance, but how they enriched our times together! For the seder is about passing on, about answering questions, about being a kind of family. The traditional seder involves answering the questions of children. It is a generational holiday, *m'dor l dor,* from one generation to the next. As we grew to middle age and older, would the seder die with us? We needed daughters.

Some brought surrogates. Lilly Rivlin often brought her young friend Naomi Wolf as her surrogate daughter.

There was to be a special Daughters' Seder in 1989. Bea pondered and chose the perfect "daughter." When her name was mentioned we smiled and nodded. She had come to us as a child. She is a college person now and takes the invitation lightly.

"Haven't heard from you," Bea reminds her, long-distance. "What's up?"

The girl isn't up for it.

Bea does not just shrug. She honors the errant maid with a rigorous lecture.

The girl weeps. "I can't hear this anymore!" and hangs up.

It's a lesson to us when we think that ours is the only show in town. Bea went to the Daughters' Seder without a "daughter."

On the other hand, for the same seder, Lilly received a call from abroad.

"I'll fly in just for the day!" the woman begs.

"For the day! It's too expensive!" says Lilly.

"It's worth it," says the older woman.

"But it's for mothers and daughters," explains Lilly.

"I'll be your daughter," implores the woman, "as you have needed to be mine."

Someone young dismisses and someone older insists.

And the older woman flew in for the day.

That third group, the guests, became an ongoing dispute.

It was 1988, at a seder in the Canadian Mission in New York where Michele Landsberg, wife of the Canadian ambassador to the United Nations, hosted us and where, for the first time, we sat around a table instead of on the floor.

Lilly Rivlin was disturbed. She had a letter to read to us. It was from a previous seder guest. This year Lilly had chosen another.

The previous guest wrote:

> Congratulations upon becoming a *Bat Mitzvah* from a woman friend who has been excluded from the ceremony. I am dismayed by the exclusivity of this event, by your following the male model of an "old girls' club." . . . If you, our elders, block out those of us who haven't been around for thirteen years, your new tradition will end with you. This is the holiday of freedom for all women, not an exclusive club. . . .
>
> I propose that each one of you . . . go . . . and organize your own Women's Seder . . . and so spread the seeds that you have planted in your private garden so that this tradition will not be stillborn.

"I feel bad about this," said Lilly.

The letter cast a pall. But what could we do? We had had as many as seventy at my loft in 1981.

"No one said anything good about that seder," said Lilly.

"Someone was drunk. It wasn't Jewish enough. It wasn't feminist enough. It was too big and impersonal."

And we had had thirteen our first year. And no one could bear to have it that small again.

How to keep it intimate and spiritual and how to pass it on?

One seder, the Seventeenth, we erred. We were told that a BBC documentary was being produced, partly in the States. The producer wanted to film a Jewish feminist event.

"No," I say.

"It's to spread the word," one of my Seder Sisters tells me.

"After," I say, "when it's all over."

I think I can keep the crew cooped up in my study and let them bring us in one at a time for interviews. But television operations are not unobtrusive.

They arrive, a crew of eight, five women and three men, with bell ringing, boom mikes, and thrusting equipment, as we're slowly trying to get to closure.

In the midst of the excitement, we forget closure. The women are distracted. Left on my washing machine in a grocery bag is the last silly, necessary item, the Sacred Schmata. With the Schmata, a pink polyester cloth, we symbolically tie ourselves together as one body of women at the end of each seder.

The crew comes out and we forget that we are bound to one another, linked in pink. The women eat quickly and rapidly leave. Michele bristles and stamps out.

It turns out that this television production is to be a three-part series whose working title is *Roots, Shmoots,* the producer tells us. It deals with his journey into his Jewish past. We seder women are just curiosities along the way.

The women are so upset no one stays for the cleanup. "Mama," Nahama reports, "some of your friends have gone to Lola's."

The Creole restaurant nearby.

Gloria Steinem and Marilyn and Jamie French are talking about the seder, the meeting of old and young, of tradition and innovation.

I sit down for chat and chatter, for laughter and the soothing of anger.

A seder needs pre-planning, the happening and post-happening. Like any sports game, analysis and gossip are all part of the mixture, the mortar.

I return to a clean kitchen. Nahama has cleared away the counter, put the dishes into the dishwasher. Though it is late at night, my Seder Sister Lilly has returned to help.

The paper bag with the Schmata is put away in my filing cabinet.

◆　◆　◆　◆

These, then, are the Seder Sisters, Mothers, Guests, and the joyful celebrations, emendations to text, and problems that confronted us through the years.

And, along the way, we made sister bonds with other women.

BELLA

It seems to me that Bella Abzug came into the group in 1979. Our theme was, "Sayings of the Mothers." We brought our mothers' sayings and recipes.

One of the invited guests was Rabbi Lynn Gottlieb, the first woman Conservative rabbi, privately given *smicha,* ordination, for the doors of the Jewish Theological Seminary had not yet opened to Conservative women rabbinical students.

Rabbi Lynn sang her own song of Miriam, the song Miriam was never allowed to sing in Exodus. Rabbi Gottlieb had developed her performance art, her sacred storytelling, by being given a congregation of the deaf. No other congregation then would hire her. For them she taught; from them she learned.

Her long brown hair hung loosely, her caftan embraced her, and her fingers shaped the words as her mouth sang a legend.

"Lovely!" said Bella, applauding.

Bella, in turn, told us of her mother, Esther.

When Bella was elected to the U.S. Congress, her mother was interviewed.

"I knew she'd make it," said Esther. "I never had to tell her to practice or to study."

Bella's father was a butcher. He named his shop the Live and Let Live Meat Market.

◆　◆　◆　◆

It was Bella's husky voice, her energetic, arm-waving singing that altered our own range. And whatever she did, it was with enthusiasm. She was at her softest when she spoke of her daughters. When they were expected at our Women's Seders, Bella would wait excitedly for the ring of the bell and rise to press the buzzer admitting them, disappointed with each newcomer, until her dark-haired girls arrived.

It was in Lilly's film, *Miriam's Daughters Now*, when the gathered are asked, "Who are the Miriams in your life? Who led you to the shore and across the sea?" that Liz Abzug turned to her mother and said, "Bella is my Miriam." Her mother blushed with pleasure.

The feeling ran in the family. I once met Bella's older sister, Helene, during a political campaign.

"My sister's one in a million," said Helene, "an exceptional person. I took a leave of absence from the school system to work on her New York senatorial campaign. She came so close! If she had won, can you imagine the difference she would have made?"

We had all admired Bella's long history of activism— defending clients before the House Un-American Activities Committee, going down to Mississippi to defend Willie McGee, the Black man accused of raping a white woman, a woman who had been his mistress. Bella fought for his case at threat to her own life. When she thinks of the political climate then, how she lost, how Willie McGee was electrocuted, she shakes her head sadly, "Yeah! Yeah!"

She had several losses at once in 1986.

Our warrior was grievously wounded. She was running in the primary from a congressional district in Westchester. She beat the Democratic candidate for Congress in the primary and was looking forward to taking her chances in the election against a lackluster Republican incumbent. Suddenly Martin, her beloved husband of forty-two years, died.

The two of them were a wicked pair, loving and teasing,

Martin more outrageous than Bella. They held hands; they had trophies from dance competitons. He was her ardent champion, a stockbroker who also secretly wrote novels. And he was gone. Bella decided, after some hesitation, to run. She lost.

At her concession speech, wonderfully dressed, smiling bravely, with her daughter Liz, the campaign manager for her mother's congressional race, on one side and Eve, a sculptor, at her other arm, she said, "Martin was always with me, all through this."

Young campaigners in the crowd began to weep.

"Be of good heart," she had the sweetness to tell them. "We shall prevail."

But she was not of good heart. She had lost heart. Lilly Rivlin had the idea for a Hug-In for Bella.

We warned Lilly, "But Bella is unsentimental. She hates touchy-feely stuff."

"What a hokey idea!" thought Michele Landsberg, whom we were just getting to know in 1986, "but when Bella started talking, my throat tightened up like an epileptic seizure. She spoke in such a restrained way. That was a successful occasion and Bella derived pleasure from it."

The Hug-In was held at Bea's loft in Westbeth, with Bella arriving, her clothing the color of wounds—a red hat, red suit, red blouse, red shoes.

Twenty-five of us gathered, all the Seder Sisters, as well as Michele Landsberg, and Naomi Newman of the Traveling Jewish Theatre.

Letty Cottin Pogrebin spoke of the past, describing Martin humorously, invoking the name that Bella could scarcely utter. Phyllis Chesler spoke of Bella's future and said Bella could do or be anything. I was assigned the present.

I said:

> . . . She has to be her size to contain it all.
> She has to be her years to know it all.
> She has to be here now to teach it all. . . .
>
> And what do we do for her in turn?
> We help her hold onto the tip of her tongue.
> We pump down the high blood pressure by serving

her only that which is salt-free, fat-free, and
    carefree.
Her too-full heart we will hold so that the
    weight of
her passions will not be too heavy for her.
And we'll all sally forth with her,
    our standard bearer.

"She carried that writing around, folded in her purse," Liz
later told me.

Naomi Newman recited a piece from her one-woman
show, *Snake Talk:*

Enough, enough of the *oi vey* path. Now, we are
going to fix it. Now we make a new way path. So,
you take a shovel . . . we are digging . . . all of a
sudden you bump into a stone. . . . You are going
to bump into lots of stones—stones of blaming,
resentment, self-pity. . . . So you bend down, you
pick them up and you throw them away.

Dig a little, pick a little, throw a little, turn yea.
Dig a little, pick a little, throw a little, turn, yea. . . .

And some people when it happens, they fall
down, and they lie there for the rest of their lives.
But some people learn how to fall down, get up.
Now that is one move. Fall-down-get-up. . . .
Okay, so now you're on your own way and you
notice that with every step you straighten up a little, and it hurts. . . . This is how you do it. You dig,
you bend down, you throw away, you go in circles
you get lost, you wait, you listen, you do nothing,
you fall down get up. . . .

Maybe there's an easier way, and, God willing,
you'll find it.

Lilly was right about that Hug-In. When it was over, Bella
swallowed, then said, "Thank you for helping me cry."

And she touched each of us lovingly.

I interviewed her for this Telling.

"Why, Bella?" I asked her. "Why, in your busy life, do you
find time to come to the Women's Seder?"

"It's a place to think and feel," she said.

And then she spoke of the Hug-In that took place some years before.

"I don't like to be hugged. Don't like to overdo. But it was so warm. It was beyond, beyond what a human being does— even I, with my enormous ego, was self-conscious at the Hug-In.

"I always experienced a tremendous amount of love from close ones—family, daughters, grandfather, mother, friends, and all the people who every day, in some way, whom I pass, whether in the day or night, come up and say loving things.

"But this was a room in which everybody was saying soothing things, in which everyone was soothing me, like lying in a pool of water. It was emotionally so giving and thoughtful."

At their best, which was frequently, at seders and in between, the Seder Sisters could restore.

In the late Spring of 1991, some weeks after our seder "The Plagues We Live Under," Bella had her Seventieth Birthday Gala. The birthday cake was in the shape of a hat.

The Seder Sisters were there in force. All the graphic art for the event was designed by Bea Kreloff.

Hundreds gathered to see Shirley MacLaine dance down the runway singing to her friend (somehow rhyming *bala-buste* with ball buster) or to watch Phil Donahue go from table to table to collect reminiscences.

Liz rises to speak. She has just been in an unsuccessful campaign for City Council. Bella was there, appearing early in the morning, at subway stops, leafleting for her daughter.

Liz had said to us, "Bella ran a dozen times. I ran once and I'm wiped out."

At the Birthday Gala, Liz remembers a childhood incident.

"When I was about nine and very headstrong, I insisted on riding a horse that was not properly broken in. The family had all gone to the country horseback riding. Bella was a fine horsewoman. Suddenly my horse began galloping away. The horse was dashing, at breakneck speed, toward a swimming pool. I held on for dear life and called for Bella.

" 'I'm coming!' she yelled, whipping her horse and gallop-ing after me.

"She came up alongside my horse and scooped me up

onto her saddle. I knew, from then on, that if I were in trouble, Bella would always save my ass."

We Seder Sisters knew that. If only the nation had realized the same. Bella is now engaged in writing her memoirs. The working title is *The Greatest Book Ever.*

EDITH

Bea had a new love. Shyly Bea showed Chesler and me her first attempts at writing love poems.

"She's beautiful," Bea told us, blushing. "She's an artist. She's Jewish."

We met her in 1979.

Edith entered the group with her married name, although she was divorced. Along the line of her time in our midst, there was a name-changing party, where Edith took her parents' first names as her last, Isaac-Rose. That meant that all her art would now have a new signature.

Being with Bea has politicized Edith's art. Before the Gulf War a group formed in the West Village, the WIMPS, Women Indicting the Military Plans and Solutions, a takeoff on President Bush's fearfulness of being called a wimp. Marching, rain or shine, through the Village, the women at first found sympathy, then accusations of being unpatriotic.

That concept of patriotism was affecting the picket signs Edith held as she marched and then became the subject of her graphics and canvases. She painted older soldiers sending the young out to war. She painted the skeletal structure underlying the costumes of men, their uniforms, whether the robe of the cleric or the bandolier's jacket with the strap across his chest filled with packets for bullets. Death and war have been her concern since the Gulf War. As she has strengthened, so has her art. After years of working abstractly, she was not afraid to change the direction of her work.

These are different concerns from the ones that earlier occupied her, the longtime married lady, summering in Fire Island or southern France, only truly her own person in her studio. She was trained to be such a married lady, as was Bea. Both had to break training. Edith was raised by emigrants fleeing Hitler who settled in that largely immigrant community of Skokie, Illinois, and became a tailor and factory-worker mother. The father was deaf, the house quiet. There were no shelves of books, no sounds of music. This offspring was a peculiar daughter for such a family, winning a scholarship to the Chicago Art Institute.

"Marry instead," encouraged her mother.

All the women had once been obedient girls. Edith did marry but, in a rare act of rebellion, finished art school. She moved where her husband moved, regardless of galleries and contacts she had developed. Friends are what comes with one's husband's work. A social wife becomes expert at the Dinner Olympics. What courage it took to fall in love with another life, her own gender, to change and accept the unacceptable.

As the Seventeenth Seder became lengthy Edith was not able to say publicly what was on her mind.

We spoke on the phone later. She was angry.

"I wanted to say how much I owe to Bea, how she has changed my work and my life."

Bea and Edith are the Jewish grandmothers among the lesbian women who have chosen to adopt or to bear children by artificial insemination, by turkey baster. They give baby showers for these couples, these singles. They baby-sit. And when we are all together, the world, it seems to me, is as good as it's going to get.

 # All of Us

SOON TO JOIN us were Grace Paley and Michele Landsberg.

It is possible to make a composite picture of my sisters. They were given limited options, marriage rather than education. They were urged by families to be less than themselves. They often came from dysfunctional families, who hardly knew why they had daughters. Some became street fighters, resisting bitterly. Others were obedient, marrying, going through decades of unhappiness until they found strength within themselves.

"It was the women's movement," Bea is sure. "What else could have done it? What other support did we have?"

Some of us had taken the traditional way, and, luckily, it worked in Letty's case, Michele's, and in mine. Others did the bidding of their teachers, their families, lost themselves along the way until they found signposts back to who they were. Still others, like Bella Abzug, set their own path, both traditional and radical.

Art helped my sisters: Lilly's photographs, her films establishing her; Bea's painting taking her out of the domestic; Edith's fine training, her excellent drawing keeping her vision clear; my writing and scholarship so that the cries of the babies were not the only sounds I heard at night. Grace Paley was the superintendent in her building in the Village when the children were little so her family could have the basement apartment free. She heard the noise from the street and translated it into poetry.

It was not a fast change for my sisters. Edith had been in a marriage for twenty-five years, Bea for twenty-four. Some were in and out of marriages, floundering, finding a family of friends to replace a family that had failed them—Lilly, for instance, in her networks of friendships. Most of us came from the working class—Gloria, Phyllis, Bea, Edith, Lilly,

Michele, and I—but privilege was no substitute for emotional support, as in the case of Letty.

At our last seder, the Seventeenth, we honored women who have altered the world for us. As her Change Makers Gloria introduced the novelist Marilyn French and scholar and writer Carolyn Heilbrun, naming them by their birth names, married names, and noms de plume.

"If I had that life, those marriages in the fifties, I never would have gotten out of it. I would not have had the strength," said Gloria, "to be who I am."

Who could incorporate so many identities?

The next group of people who joined us came to us in strength.

What united us as well as those to come was activism.

Some of us were pacifists but not passive, like Grace Paley. All of us were of the body politic. Some were journalists, like Gloria and Letty of *Ms.* magazine or Michele Landsberg, a featured columnist for the *Toronto Star.* Phyllis Chesler wrote muckraking feminist books that took on the health profession and the legal profession. Some of us were involved in international politics, like Bella Abzug and Grace Paley. Letty involves herself in peace efforts between Israelis and Palestinians and serves on the board of Peace Now.

Activism was our creed.

"Let politics be your *halacha,* righteous religious action!" Michele Landsberg exhorted us one seder.

Bella Abzug, always at the forefront, was even willing to rewrite the past.

"Get new foremothers," she said that same seder, impatient with the quarreling between our ancestors, Sarah and Hagar, Rachel and Leah. "These are only male constructs!"

We were all seasoned marchers. Some of us remembered the days of the Sixties and the Antiwar Movement with nostalgia, as a time of firm tread and firm thighs.

GRACE

One who came to us from the Eighth Seder on was Grace Paley.

"I was extremely eager to go," said Grace. "I was very interested in it. I also felt somewhat outside of it. That feeling went away the next time I went. I felt like everybody knew what to say and I didn't know what to say. Everybody had been thinking about what to do, not I. I had just thought about coming."

It was a Kabbalistic seder, concentrating on the Number Eight.

Guests were speaking of the symbolism of eight, the yin and yang of it, then it was Grace's turn.

"It took eight hours for me to get down to the seder from my farm in Vermont," Grace cracked.

Grace, with the sweetest face among us, the earthiest, the one with the least artifice and the most art, was thoughtful about the seders. "I love the process," she said. As long as people think they're discovering from and working toward that process and trying to understand our relationship as Jewish women to the history and life of our people, it's a wonderful thing and should go on."

Grace was raised in an extended family. Like Bella, she was loved by all, the youngest, the pet, of father, grandmother, oldest sister, aunts, and brother. She learned, in a household of vociferously differing views, her great tolerance. There were no two opinions alike in that family, but Grace learned to listen to one side, to the other, and to love all without reservation.

We were all fans of Grace, of her literature and her activism. We would show up regularly anytime she read in the area or had a book-signing party. We think of her as "the Boss of Peace" and attend every action she assigns.

"I was amazed by Grace," Michele told me, "whose writing I have adored, and when she came into our seder and talked in that same voice as in her stories, I was so happy to find it all so authentic."

We had attended Grace's sixty-fifth birthday party to benefit the War Resisters' League, where her files, recovered from the state or FBI undercover intelligence agencies, were read aloud to great laughter and applause. Her many years of courageous involvement were revealed by the words of her opponents.

Like Bea, like Bella, Grace was filled with love and support, which she passed on, personally, politically. Her growing up years were good training for an activist and pacifist. She would refer to the settling of disputes in her family when we held our Seder of Intra-Group Mediation.

I remember going to her trial.

"Better come see me in Washington," said Grace, "because I don't know the results. I could be jailed for some time."

She was part of a group of anti-nuclear protesters who eventually came to be known as Washington Eleven. In 1977 they unfurled a banner on the White House Lawn during the Carter administration ("No more nuclear armaments, USA/USSR"). Simultaneously, a group of Americans unfurled the same banner in Red Square in the Soviet Union. The protesters in the Soviet Union were merely deported. Though Carter had run for president on an anti-nuclear platform, the Washington protesters were arrested, charged not with trespassing but with unlawful entry, jailed for thirty hours, and eventually brought to trial.

I was living then in Detroit and flew to the nation's Capitol through a rare snowstorm in D.C. The courtroom was changed when Judge Smith saw it crowded with friends and supporters as well as Paley's colleagues and students from Sarah Lawrence College. The new courtroom would accommodate only a much smaller audience.

"Count yourselves off," said a stern guard, "and choose who is to stay and who is to leave."

Many reluctantly left. I stubbornly stayed.

"Why did you do this act?" Judge Smith asked Grace Paley.

"We were trying to speak beyond the range of our own voices," said Grace. "We stepped onto the grass in order to be heard. We made sure how we could do the simplest, gentlest, quietest way the thing we set out to do. I had bare arms. We walked slowly. We had nothing in our hands. We did not want to threaten. It was the police who made the event threatening."

"When will you stop?" asked the judge.

"I'm getting old. Pretty soon, I'll stop."

She never stopped.

"You see, Your Honor," said Grace, "there is a war against my city. Every time weaponry is built, the cities suffer. New

York suffers. We have to stop building armament and build cities instead."

Her probation required three years of not engaging in political activity in the nation's capitol. In the meantime, the Women's Pentagon Action evolved, for the Pentagon was in Maryland and Paley was not prohibited from marching in Maryland.

When Paley was once again allowed in D.C., I accompanied her on one of her innumerable marches. When the protest ended, Grace said, "Wait just a minute for me, and we'll take the train back to New York together."

She was to spend another hour or two kissing good-bye friends lined up at the march. I returned to the city alone.

There were those among us filled with love, whose battles were not internecine, but of larger matter. Grace was one, Michele was another.

MICHELE

Michele Landsberg is short-haired, ample, literate, and wicked in humor. Her laughter is throaty from chain-smoking.

She is the last to join the group.

"I had already heard about your *Women's Haggadah,* which I tore out (of *Ms.*) and was thrilled with," Michele said. "I had been making the seder with no help. I had no traditional Jewish upbringing. Stephen had no Jewish upbringing."

What Stephen Lewis had, though, was a thoroughly political upbringing. His father, David Lewis, had founded the New Democratic Party in Canada and become its national leader, and Stephen was the provincial leader from Toronto. Michele is committed to the party. In the film *Half the Kingdom,* in which several of us are shown, Michele is campaigning door-to-door for the NDP.

In *Half the Kingdom* Michele also describes her childhood in Canada and how the Holocaust was never discussed but the children were brought up with strict instructions not to look or act Jewish.

"We were passing for white," said Michele, staring sternly into the camera.

There was some reason for this. A Canadian official, when requested to admit Jewish refugees fleeing from Germany, was quoted as having said, "One is too many."

Michele's mother worked and suffered the condemnation of the Holy Blossom Reform Temple for being a working wife. Her father was a handsome traveling salesman, but it was her mother who was Michele's supporter. Michele once said that the only time her mother struck her was when she used slang. "Speak English correctly!" her mother commanded. And Michele's English is more than correct. It is elegant.

Michele schooled herself rigorously and wanted to pursue a doctorate at the University of Toronto, only to be ridiculed for it by the Canadian writer, her professor at the university, Robertson Davies.

"When I see young women who get their doctorates, it thrills me," she said, "because I was not allowed to."

What she has become is the leading feminist columnist in Canada. One *Toronto Star* columnist told me, "Landsberg is my touchstone. I read her three times a week for sanity."

When Gloria Steinem and I were on a panel in Toronto in 1992 with Michele, the audience gave Michele a standing ovation.

"We wanted her to come back to us to New York," Gloria told the audience, "but I see you have a right to her. She is a national treasure."

Michele did not think of herself as a national treasure, especially in her early years when she wrote a daily column for the *Toronto Globe and Mail,* had three children, and ran her household. Hers was the only feminist voice in town. And she was very much alone in her efforts and convictions as a woman and as a Jew.

She discovered feminist rituals in 1977, while doing her traditional duties.

"I had to run back and forth from the kitchen doing the Passover service, doing the cooking, and that was a lot of work. And over the years I was disturbed by the masculinist language, but I had not the courage or the energy (to change it) and there (*The Women's Haggadah*) was. Afterward, I incorporated *The Women's Haggadah* into the service."

Out of her country, away from her natural habitat, she found more like souls in New York.

"I was so thrilled that somewhere there was a community of like-minded sisters. That first intimation gave me courage to go on. I felt that there was a real life in the universe, little radio bleeps were going out into the cosmos. That's why New York is my Jerusalem!" says Michele, never short on enthusiasm.

The difference between her Canadian life and her New York years was simply that in New York, "People formulate ideas and act on them," but, "In Toronto, everybody is alone, in their corner. It's very difficult to grow that way. No peer group struggled for women of our age, in Canada, so our identity was always diluted rather than strengthened. It's best when it's with friends and peer groups."

Michele seems, at the same time, to be young and giggly and middle-aged, earthy and earnest. Michele Landsberg had to be a proper wife, in part, when she first came to New York to join her husband, His Excellency Stephen Lewis, Canadian ambassador to the United Nations. It was not all easy.

"My first year in New York I got to know the ambassadorial women and discovered the amount of anti-Semitism at the UN. I made little stabs at getting to know people."

She was lonely at first but an intrepid explorer, continuing to send back weekly columns about the visitor in New York for the *Toronto Star.*

One of her columns came about because of her neighborhood. The Canadian Mission is located in the East Sixties, off Park Avenue. Ambassadors from other lands often stay at nearby hotels.

One day, looking out of her window, she hears a roar and hissing sounds. She opens the window a crack and her kitten tries to crawl out on the sill. Michele closes the window, but not before seeing a swarming crowd of black-coated Hasidim cursing.

"Peres," they curse the then Israeli Minister of Foreign Affairs, a liberal statesman. "Peres is a Nazi!"

Although wearing a cotton housedress in this elegant building that also houses the former managing editor of *Vogue* magazine, Diane Vreeland, Michele marches out of the apartment, takes the elevator to the lobby and plunges into the crowd. The doormen and elevator operator come out to watch her, dumbfounded.

"It's a *shandeh,* a shame," she bawls them out. "Shame on you! Peace Now!" she shouts and makes the V for Victory sign.

The black coats begin swirling around her, their side curls shaking, as they crowd in next to her. To each she continues saying, "Shame. *Feh!*"

And then she sees a blue-clad arm extended and hears a voice saying, "May I help you, Madam?"

He escorts her out of the crowd and she marches with him, head held high, still calling back, "*Feh! Shandeh!*" And making the peace sign.

The employees of the apartment house greeted her warmly.

Stephen, when he hears of the afternoon's doings, says, "That's your next column."

◆　◆　◆　◆

In 1985 or '86, Michele met our group through a typical New York way of connecting, a fund-raiser.

"You introduced yourself," she reminded me, "at the fund-raiser in your loft. It was to raise monies to send Marcia Freedman to Israel to research and complete her book, *Exile in the Promised Land.*

"Everyone was welcoming and forthcoming and I felt like I was home. I thought I had died and gone to heaven.

"You said, 'Enjoy. Here's an apple. Eat.' I saved the apple you gave me and took it to my daughter Ilana in Toronto. She had first introduced me to your work.

"Lilly Rivlin called. Then others. The group at the loft I didn't at first connect to the Feminist Seder. Gradually it filtered through to me that this was the group that did the seder!"

The second time we met Michele as a group was at an impromptu Canadian women's film festival she held at the Canadian Mission, where the Ambassador's family was in residence. (No *mazuzahs* allowed on the doorpost that would offend visiting Muslim delegations.)

Under the Liberal Party, the Canadian Film Board was supportive of the arts. Studio Four was especially supportive of women documentary filmmakers. With the Conservative Government the support lessened considerably.

The night of the private showing, Bea, Edith, Lilly, and I saw four Canadian women's films. At midnight, bleary-eyed, we staggered to the door. Stephen Lewis was returning from a late-night UN meeting.

"Honey," said Michele grandly to Stephen, "meet my coven."

The next year, 1987, Michele became a Seder Sister.

"The Seder Sisters," said Michele, "were an integral part of being in New York. I felt so in harmony. With all their difficulty and their quarrels, which had been evident to me, yet I felt an instant bond. We are all passionate feminists who praise, extol, uphold each other.

"I had never been in a consciousness-raising group. There had never been a chance in Canada. I felt at home in New York because of the Seder Sisters."

Is Michele religious?

"The spiritual part was not in me. I understand reverence and awe but not belief. However, the seder is as close as I could get to religious experience. Amazing to insert yourself into it!"

And her plans for the future?

Flying into New York every Passover.

"I hope I'll always be at the seder. One of my crowning laurels is to be a Seder Sister."

Michele's New York experiences, including her "terrorizing" of the Hasidim, are described in *This Is New York, Honey* (Toronto: McClelland and Stuart, 1989), which topped the best-seller list in Canada.

▓ Spiritual Wrangling

1992

We called ourselves nothing in the beginning, not knowing
there would be continuity and a need for nomenclature.

We were like the Elders of the Haggadah who answered
the questions of the children, and we were also the Four
Children: the Wise, the Disaffected, the Simple, and the
Ignorant. Perhaps, after a while, we stereotyped our roles
into a different four: the Ambitious, the Competitive, the
Searcher, and the Social.

Can a group of such disparate women create community
and magic? It seemed as if the different elements in the
process did come together to perform the Theater of
Spirituality. The Contrary became obliging, the Hostile gen-
tled out of anger, the Ambitious sharing, the Simple wiser.
And often we took turns being each of these participants,
these children.

"The miracle is," said my son Adam, when I recounted to
him the occasional acrimony and differences, "that the
Contrary is never kept out of the seder, not in the traditional
Haggadah and not with the Seder Sisters. Nor is the Simple.
Nor even the One Who Does Not Know How to
Participate. They are all accepted and expected to return."

Even if one were bawled out in the seder group, spoken to
derisively or condescendingly, were herself the source of
contention, we each, in our idiosyncracy, were tolerated. As
in a kibbutz we learned that in order to make our basic product—Holiday—we had to negotiate, have our *pegishot,* meetings, and our *sichot,* conversations.

At other spiritual or feminist events, I have seen this contention and negotiation duplicated.

I was at the Timbrels of Miriam conference at the
University of Judaism, 1991, and heard that everyone among
the planners wanted to be Miriam, singing her own song at

the seashore, shaking her tambourine the loudest. The planners, therefore, distributed several "timbrels," each with a different participant's name on it.

At a panel discussion in Toronto, April 1, 1992, with Gloria Steinem, Michele Landsberg, and me, the audience raised disturbing questions. The event was a fund-raiser for a film to be made of my novel, *A Weave of Women*.

"We need a community of women to raise the money for a film about a community of women," said the producer, Francine Zuckerman.

Such a community of brave volunteers did indeed appear, responsible for the sellout audience in the auditorium.

During the question-and-answer time, a woman in the back of the auditorium rose.

"Is there always so much bad feeling, so much wrangling and competition in our circles, even when we're feminists working for a common cause?" Gloria, Michele, and I looked rueful. That had been part of our experience, though the other part far outweighed the niggling, the nagging. Even spiritual people were killers when it came to publicity and *koved,* honor.

"I'll quote Letty Cottin Pogrebin," I answered the questioner, "who said, 'There are not enough chairs of honor for women.'

"Sometimes we sit on each other's laps, both trying to squeeze into the same chair," I added.

The questioner slowly returned to her seat, hoping, perhaps, to find a feminist game of musical chairs in which there would be enough seats for everyone.

In Toronto, in 1992, there is a First Feminist Seder.

"We brought 'Grandmother Baskets,' " Francine Zuckerman explained to me, "baskets filled with family artifacts. There was a sharing of stories, family stories, Passover and Easter tales. Someone brought along a guitar and we were up singing until 3:00 A.M."

In our early seders no one mentioned hunger or the passing of time. We were so high on discovery.

Michele showed me another kind of basket, a Purim basket, for the First Feminist Purim with Michele Landsberg's group, the *Schvesters.*

Over the traditional Book of Esther, Michele had taped a raunchy transformation, the New Scroll of Esther. Esther forms a consciousness-raising group with the former Queen Vashti and the other women in the harem in revolt against the king and his prime minister Haman, and the women triumph. In Michele's *schalach munot,* basket of gifts, traditional at that holiday, were *greigers,* noisemakers, that made the loud grinding sound when the villains of the holiday were mentioned, tinkling bells when the heroines' names were spoken aloud. And there were *hamentashen,* three-cornered, poppy seed–filled tarts, and a bottle of champagne.

Landsberg is a new kind of Little Red Riding Hood. Or Robin Hood, stealing from the old tradition to make the new one.

"The *Schvesters* were convulsed," said Michele. "They learned they can make a holiday their own."

But not the New York Seder Sisters.

"The natives are restless," warns Michele in Toronto. "I hear the beating of the drums from here."

Am I losing control of the seder? What part am I to play?

"Next year is our Eighteenth, our *Hai,* Life," says Lilly. "We should rent a hall, charge admission, and show everyone how to hold a seder."

"Oh no," I object. "We should have an intimate one, just ourselves."

Michele, a peace person, has a unique suggestion. She thinks of Israel and Peace Now as a paradigm. She would exchange, she tells me, "turf for peace," "territory for continuity." She sends out a letter to the group.

"Instead of wrangling over who gets honoured, who gets to invite whom, and who sits in the place of chief rabbi, I propose that we plan an extremely small seder. . . .

"Let's make a heroic effort to set aside rancour, division, personal ego. . . .

"To me, the great distinguishing strength of the feminist seder has always been the coherence and poetic beauty with which it is written. . . . We could re-affirm our joint determination to create a kind of Jewish observance that puts *woman* at the centre."

Michele refers to the past year when we forgot our funny emblem, the Sacred Schmata, and left it, neglected, in its paper bag on top of my washing machine.

Michele concludes her letter:

"Could we end the Seder this year with the Sacred Shmata, bound together with true emotion?"

Lilly, large-spirited and inclusive, phones.

"I had better get my letter to the Seder Sisters into the mail."

So we write and fax and phone and, hopefully, negotiate our way through the thorny path of hurt feelings and large expectations.

It makes me think that sometimes even feminists have a certain need to preside, order, and control, rather than working by consensus.

I thought of a trip I took with Gloria Steinem and of our conversation.

Gloria and I fly from Toronto to New York, after the fund-raiser of Spring '92. Although it is an early flight, 7:00 A.M., Gloria and I manage to hold a conversation.

Gloria says of one of the Seder Sisters, "The problem with her is she thinks there is a right and a wrong. And you know there's more to it than that. And she also thinks that if you organize, it will all turn out. But there is a certain disorganization that has to occur in organization."

She could be talking about me, as well.

Gloria, in the middle of her busy book tour selling *Revolution from Within* (Boston: Little, Brown, 1992), reminds me that we have to learn not to be linear and controlling, that what we have been taught to value—orderliness, organizational ability, judgmentalism—may not be so useful after all.

That may not be the way women will have to learn to work together.

 # The Symbolist

PERHAPS THE OPPOSITE of Gloria's discussion of the orderly, organized behavior of some of us, is the organic, passionate behavior of Phyllis Chesler.

This is not to imply that she lacks discipline. She reads a book a night, which she can summarize cogently in the morning. She has total recall, besides her wit and humor. She is outrageous also.

Lilly and I often recall an evening with Phyllis at the Village Gate. Phyllis had been in an auto accident; her hands had been operated on and were in casts. We women were out for dinner and pop tunes.

"Does anybody in the audience want to sing?" the pianist at the Village Gate asked.

Phyllis jumped up.

She whispered her request to the musician.

And then she began singing in a surprisingly rich and sweet voice. The song was, "Embraceable You," which she belted out, holding her two hands in casts before her, not able to connect them or to embrace.

◆　◆　◆　◆

When Phyllis is working under contract, she neither eats nor sleeps until the manuscript is complete. And she is passionate about causes; during Mary Beth Whitehead's trial in New Jersey for custody of her child, Phyllis traveled to New Jersey daily, even organizing rituals like rocking empty cradles to symbolize the baby that had been removed from Whitehead's breast and given to the sperm donor.

When Phyllis began, as a therapist, counseling clients who had lost custody of their children, or had gone underground, rescuing children from abusive fathers, Phyllis saw the need for a book and wrote, *Mothers on Trial: The Battle for Children*

& *Custody* (New York: McGraw Hill, 1986). She testified at Congressional Hearings and held a conference in New York at John Jay College where the women movingly testified.

As she is capable of passion, tenderness, sweetness, she is equally capable of righteous anger and wrath.

Yet, there is that to her which some would call the Priestess, a kind of Oracle, a woman who works symbolically and metaphorically.

THE SACRED SCHMATA

The Sacred Schmata was her idea—and its almost-demise—also hers.

For our Eighth Seder, Phyllis tied together yards of pink polyester curtainy material. With this schlocky fabric, she told us to bind ourselves together. We passed the pink rope among us, around us, through us. It just reached around us all, connecting, knotting us to one another. We resolved to be thus connected, tied to ceremony and tradition, whatever our background and religion.

"I thought of this as silly at first," says Michele, "but then it came to be delightful and I looked forward to its appearance every year."

Before the Ninth Seder, Phyllis brought the material over to my loft in a brown paper grocery bag. Lilly Rivlin and I were going on a pilgrimage. A group called the Doughnuts, children of great wealth, had organized a spiritual meeting in the Sinai. There, on what is now Egyptian territory, certain selected people of faith would meet to hear each others' tales and prayers. I was to go and requested that Lilly, a person who builds bridges between peoples, accompany me.

For luck, and to tie the disparate group together, Phyllis made the trip from Brooklyn, handed over our artifact, kissed us each on both cheeks and wished us well on the trip.

At the Ninth Seder, Lilly hired a film crew. With little financial backing, collecting, as she puts it, "nickels and dimes," she put the film together.

There we are at the seder sitting with the Sacred Schmata, explaining to the congregants in the large gathering that this polyester had bound together witnesses.

Lilly and I had performed a woman's ritual, of getting the women of Egypt and the women of Israel to pledge not to bloody the sands of the desert with war. We tied together the surrounding body of priests, ministers, rabbis, mullahs as witnesses to this pledge of peace between formerly warring countries.

From then on, every year, with great flair, Chesler would pull the Sacred Schmata out of its bag. Until, one seder, at the Canadian Mission, 1987 or '88, Chesler felt we no longer needed an external object for empowerment.

"We are asking for empowerment within ourselves," she proclaimed.

Since the Schmata was "external power that weakened" us, Chesler hurled it into the fireplace in Michele's spacious living room.

Suddenly, Letty burst into tears and snatched the Schmata from the flames.

"I lost so much," she said after, "with my mother dying when I was so young. I lost all her things. I could not bear losing again."

It was decreed that Letty be the Keeper of the Schmata, and it returned home with her still in its brown paper bag.

One seder, the Daughters' Seder, Letty arrived at her daughters's apartment, where the seder would be held, carrying bags of food.

"You have the Schmata?" I asked.

Instantly, Bert Pogrebin and Letty returned midtown to pick up the bag and drive once more all the way uptown.

The Daughters' Seder ended with the mothers and daughters and surrogate daughters wrapped together around wrists and waists, by the Schmata, singing the song to welcome Miriam the Prophet. We used the Sacred Schmata from 1983 until its temporary neglect in 1992, but it was in the desert of the Sinai in 1984 and linking the generations in 1989 that the Schmata became something transcendent, golden twine, a tie that bound us, it seemed then, permanently.

THE TENT

After Lilly and I had spent time in the desert in 1984, living in tents, in The Sinai Gathering, Phyllis conceived of using tent-like coverings for our Ninth Seder.

"This tent," she said, "is for ourselves and for women still in the desert spiritually, politically. Women are among the homeless," she reminded us.

She had brought table clothes and spreads for us. We held them high over our heads as a roof. We were housed. Rivlin's film, *Miriam's Daughters Now,* ends with the cloths reaching from one end of the seder group to the other, all across my husband's long studio, sheltering us.

APPLE, STONE, WATER, CORN

Lilly Rivlin and I performed our "New Year on the Pier" during the High Holy Days, over the Hudson River. We performed this *Tashlich,* the casting off of sins from the previous year, into the water. For seven years, we invited our sisters to participate in the ceremony of throwing away their "sins," or what had been deemed sinful or burdensome. It was also a time of asking one another for forgiveness of any wrongdoing during the year. Lilly and I wrote prayers for this holiday, which ended under a *talith,* a group prayer shawl. The *talith* was a tablecloth of Lilly's late grandmother, made sacred by the stains of life. Covered by this tablecloth, the women on the edge of the pier shouted in the New Year.

At one of these gatherings Chesler brought an apple.

"We should all eat of the apple of Eve," she said, "and gain wisdom. Take a good bite!" she ordered.

We did eat Eve's apple, round, red, full to its core, going around the group.

Water, said Chesler, was Miriam's symbol. To honor Miriam at another seder, our Sixteenth, Chesler brought pottery cups for water.

"This is Miriam and all the women at the well," said Phyllis. "Let us drink from their well."

And the cups went from lip to lip.

Phyllis had prepared ears of corn for the Seventh Seder. Corn was the symbol of the Earth Goddess, Demeter, often portrayed holding an ear of corn. Chesler also referred to the biblical story of Joseph, who was asked to interpret the Pharaoh's dream. There were seven years of full corn and seven of dried corn, dreamed Pharaoh. Joseph said that were would be seven years of plenty, followed by the seven years of drought.

"It is now the beginning of the seven years of drought," said Chesler.

Her predictions in 1982 proved to be true.

"Chesler is oracular," Michele had proclaimed.

THE NEW TEN COMMANDMENTS

In 1985 Phyllis brought two guests to the seder. One was a psychiatrist, Teresa Bernardez, who founded the Feminist Psychoanalytic Institute in East Lansing, Michigan, and the other was Deborah Luepnitz, a therapist from Philadelphia. They had a modest task: rewriting *The Ten Commandments.*

THE TEN COMMANDMENTS (IN PART)

LOVE THY SISTER AS YOU LOVE YOURSELF.

LOVE AND CHERISH YOUR MOTHER AND ALL WHO ARE GOOD TO HER.

PRESERVE LIFE AND USE ANGER TO PRESERVE IT.

THOU SHALT TAKE BACK WHAT HAS BEEN STOLEN FROM US, AND SHARE IT JOYOUSLY.

TELL THE TRUTH IN A LOUD VOICE AND IN WHISPERS.

CELEBRATE IN YOUR SISTERS WHAT MEN WOULD HAVE YOU ENVY IN THEM.

HEED NOT THESE WORDS AS THOUGH CARVED IN STONE.

There must be somewhere a symbol that confers permanent honor, constant laurels upon the symbolist herself.

## PART TWO

The Laden Table

The Laden Table

IN MY MOTHER'S household, as well as my own, the festive meal at Passover was predictable: chicken soup with matzo balls; gefilte fish—homemade in mother's house, out of a jar in mine; potato kugel; carrot *tsimmis*—a sweet dish of honeyed carrots, apricots, and apples; followed by a sponge cake made from potato starch and tea.

We, at the Women's Seder, had a more varied menu, some of us vegetarians, others macrobiotic, besides the kosher kids among us.

There was always a flock of boiled, fried, or roasted chickens. But one offering of chicken soup, hard to bring, was a dramatic contribution to the meal that I still remember.

It was 1978, the Seder of the Just Woman, held at Westbeth, the New York housing for artists and theater and dance tenants. I found myself following Rosetta Reitz down the corridor. She was the music publisher of African-American women's jazz and blues. She brought a cauldron of steaming chicken soup with floating matzo balls. I followed this spilling, slippery potion down the corridors of Westbeth to Bea's apartment. There was something witchlike, with this dark-haired woman and her black, swinging cauldron, steaming up the hallway as we moved on toward the gathering.

On the night of the women's seder, the planners dress elaborately for the holiday and for one another.

We have assignments. Usually Bella and I roast chickens and Bea and Edith roast a turkey. Lilly Rivlin often cooks, "with inspirational love," a vegetable dish.

"One year I made *meichels*," Lilly remembers. *Meichels* is a pleasurable offering, usually referring to food. "You *potch* around and put all sorts of things together with love, with your very being. One year I had a layer of sweet potatoes, a layer of yellow squash, green squash, a layer of carrots, spinach. I went for color. I only get like that when I'm doing something for people I love."

Another year, before our 1988 seder, Lilly made a Healing Ceremony to try to clear the air between us. For that she made a Passover soup with beans, peas, mushrooms.

"It was made out of impulsive love," said Lilly.

The soup worked wonderfully well, the healing less so, but more of that later on.

The Seventeenth Seder, in 1992, Lilly returned to colorful dishes, layers of sweet potatoes and carrots for a carrot *tsimmis.*

We alternate bringing the seder plate with its symbols of bitterness and rebirth, sometimes Lilly or Letty or I, or, one wonderful year when the daughters made the seder, they composed the plate and gave a new interpretation to the symbols on the plate.

The year of the Daughters' Seder, Nahama worried that the mothers would be undependable and not bring enough food. So she brought bags of vegetables from Balducci's gourmet market and painstakingly cut them into small pieces for an Israeli salad. The mothers arrived in taxis and left the cabs staggering under bowls and pans.

"There was hardly a dent in the salad," Nahama mourned.

Letty's files still have her list of assignments for one of the seders; 1979, the Fourth: "Susan Brownmiller brought the sponge cake," she had noted, "Eve Merriam, gefilte fish; Gloria Steinem, kosher wine; Bella Abzug, chicken."

Letty remembers, "They didn't have enough wine that first time. We ran out. And now I'm always phoning people ahead of time to make sure there's enough wine."

By the Fifteenth Seder, 1990, with much to distract her—probably the writing of her memoir, *Deborah, Golda, and Me*—Letty arrived at Bea's without her assignment, the *haroseth,* the nut-apple-wine mixture to represent the mortar, that which was denied the Hebrew slaves who worked on the pyramids. All the guests waited. Quickly, Robin and Abigail were dispatched to the beautiful Korean vegetable market a block from Westbeth, picked up the necessary ingredients, and, with the help of the Cuisinart, we were ready with only a slight delay.

The very first seder Gloria arrived at Phyllis's apartment with a cake, neatly boxed and tied.

"Is it a Passover cake?" asked someone worriedly.

"It's from a very good bakery," Gloria said.

She did not know that Passover cakes are made from special ingredients.

"Thank you," said Phyllis graciously, taking the box from Gloria's hands, and putting it into her freezer until the eight days of Passover ended.

From then on, Gloria was assigned to bring Passover sanctified wine, though recently seltzer was added to her load.

Claudia Weinstein, then about twenty-two, was invited to the Ninth Seder, the seder that Lilly would film.

"Do we need anything?" she asked politely.

I was making up the seder plate.

I looked around wildly. "Where are the matzoth?"

Claudia and Bea rushed out for matzoth, without which there would have been no seder.

One year Grace Paley was assigned vegetables. She prepared an asparagus dish with a special dressing and carried it carefully the few blocks from her Village apartment to my loft. She rang the bell. It was noisy and no one heard the bell. She went to the corner telephone booth to call. We had the phone ringer turned off. Grace returned to her apartment, which she shared with a roommate when Grace came into town from her farm in Vermont.

"She was rather surprised, if not annoyed, to see me returning," said Grace mildly. "But we sat quietly and ate my offering."

We still grieve that loss of Grace as well as the asparagus.

For the Eighth Seder, Lucy Lippard, the distinguished art critic, besides bringing her theme of the yin and yang of the number eight, also brought a flat of sweet strawberries.

Sometimes guests get so carried away they arrive with huge wheels of fruit, cheeses, vegetable platters.

On April 15, 1992, the counter in my loft was laden. Edith Konecky, novelist, brought chopped chicken liver made with schmaltz. Marilyn French cooked two chickens in broth.

One morning Marilyn and her mother had spoken on the phone, miles apart.

"I've discovered a new way of preparing chicken," said Marilyn.

"I have, also," said her mother.

It turned out to be the same recipe they each had invented.

MARILYN FRENCH'S POACHED CHICKEN

Cut chicken into pieces
Chicken may or may not be browned. If not
browned, but dry, pour broth over pieces, sear at a
boil.
Broth, 24 oz. per chicken, or 4 cups

Put in:
1½" bits of carrots and celery
whole head of onion
parsley chopped fine, dill, rosemary

Bring to a boil, then simmer for 45–50 minutes
until tender.
Optional: noodles or potatoes

Marilyn French also found this dish, with cream added, in a convent in Belgium.

Michele Landsberg and her daughter, Jenny Lewis, bought purple plastic bowls and filled them with fruit from Balducci's, topped with floral decoration, to celebrate the Seventeenth Seder.

Bella has a special dish from her mother Esther. She gave the recipe one year to the *New York Daily News:*

BELLA ABZUG'S MEAT LATKES,
FROM HER MOTHER ESTHER

2 cups mashed potatoes
¼ cup matzoh cake meal
2 beaten eggs
salt and pepper to taste
1 cup ground liver or other meat
schmaltz

Combine potatoes, cake meal, eggs, and seasoning,
and shape into ½" balls. Scoop a hole in the center
of each ball and fill it with ground meat. Press the
potato mixture over the top and flatten. Fry in the
schmaltz.

By the Seventeenth Seder, Bella was avoiding schmaltz, chopped liver, fried foods, all that her mother Esther would have considered an essential part of the festive meal.

Lilly's film, *Miriam's Daughters Now,* shows us gathering and piling the table high, a groaning board.

After the lengthy ceremony, we have earned the meal. We fill our plates, find a place to sit in an intimate group or enter in a larger circle, critiquing the event as if it were a play and we the reviewers, loving one another and marveling that for yet another year we managed to make holiday.

## PART THREE

# The Old and New Order

 The Old Order

THE PARENT BEFORE the child, the old before the new, tradition before innovation.

The Passover Haggadah begins with the searching for leaven, after the final preparation for Passover. One places bread or packets of crumbs around the house. Leaven must be found or there could be no prayer said over the leaven that will be burned the following morning: "Any leaven . . . shall be as if it does not exist, and as the dust of the earth."

The table is set and in the center are two dishes and a cup. One plate contains three matzoth wrapped in cloth, the middle one given special significance. That is the *afikomen, gift* in Greek, which is divided in half and one half hidden. The hidden matzo must be discovered by the children after the meal so the seder can continue. The adults then bargain with the children to redeem the *afikomen*. Perhaps this custom has to do with completion, with the two parts of the seder connected by the older and the younger members. The symbology is lost in antiquity.

There is the specially designed and decorated seder dish with its egg, shank bone, bitter herbs, parsley, and *haroseth*. Next to the plates is a cup containing salted water.

One recites the order of the seder, that is, the Blessing; washing of hands; eating a green vegetable; breaking the middle matzo and hiding it as the *afikomen;* reciting the Passover tale; washing hands; saying the prayer for the matzo; eating the bitter herb, the bitter herb sandwich, the festival meal; the finding and eating of the *afikomen;* grace after meal; Hallel, praises; and conclusion.

The recitation of *Siman L'Seder Shel Pesach,* the Order of the Passover Seder, makes it seem as if every item on the list were of equal importance and equal length. Eating a green vegetable or washing the hands is not as lengthy or thoughtful a task as reciting the Passover story.

As with the aforementioned order, the sedergoers com-
mence to bless the wine. (If the seder is on Friday night,
there is a special addition of Shabbat prayers.)

One performs the tasks prescribed above, and soon one
comes to the Passover story, beginning with the famous, "*Ha
Lachma Anya.* This is the bread of affliction which our forefathers ate in the land of Egypt."

The hungry and needy are invited to join the celebration.

The Passover plate is displayed, set down, and the youngest
child present asks the four questions: Why is unleavened
bread eaten on this night? Why bitter herbs on this night?
Why do we dip the herbs (into saltwater)? Why do we
recline as we tell the tale?

The answers indirectly deal with the questions. The bitter
herbs are for the plagues inflicted on our enemies, for we
mourn for their travail as well; leaning is to show that the congregants are free and can proceed in a leisurely fashion. There
are another four questions by four sons, whose attributes vary
from clever to wicked to simple to uncomprehending.

Again there is a discursive response, often interrupted with
pilpul, minutia, such as, Do days also constitute nights?

But as the narrative progresses, one learns that the Hebrew
ancestors once worshiped idols, then, with Abraham, left the
land "beyond the river" to go to Canaan, where they
increased. Then on to Egypt, where they were oppressed.
"And the Egyptians did evil unto us." "But the Eternal heard
our voice." The tribe was brought out of Egypt with signs of
(1) Blood, (2) Fire, (3) Pillars of Smoke.

The plagues are called out at this point, increasing in
horror until the final, terrible Slaying of the Firstborn, all
inflicted on the Egyptians.

There is then singing of thanks to God, for the deeds God
performed for the tribe. Each in itself would have sufficed:
"Had He brought us out from Egypt, *Dayenu,* it would have
sufficed. . . . Had He divided the sea for us, *Dayenu.* . . . Had
He helped us forty years in the desert, *Dayenu.* . . . Had He
brought us to the Land of Israel / and not built for us the
Holy Temple, *Dayenu.*"

One then describes the Passover Offering; the Matzo, the

Bitter Herbs, and Lamb Shank. One sings psalms, drinks the second cup of wine, performs the actions that precede the festival meal.

The meal is the highlight, much worked on. The cupboards, in more observant families, have been cleared out; the Passover dishes and pots and pans, in storage all year, are brought out.

There is the serving of the Festival Meal, made of Passover ingredients.

Soon one drinks the third cup of wine, fills the fourth cup.

One calls out to God, the troubling, "Pour out Thy wrath upon the nations that know Thee not . . . for they have consumed Jacob and laid waste his habitation. . . . " There is an awkwardness among some of us in cursing those who "know Thee not," who have other Gods.

The door is opened for the prophet Elijah to drink from the fourth cup. Children are often given this task and told to watch the table for the drinking of the cup by the invisible prophet.

After the meal and before the service continues, the hidden *afikomen* is bought back and eaten.

There are more psalms of praise and the singing of the familiar songs: "It Happened at Midnight!" and the counting songs of "Who knows One?" and *Had Gadya,* "One Little Goat." The latter song is a listing from the most helpless to the most powerful, from the goat to the slaughterer to the angel of death to the Holy One, from the powerless to the almighty.

The seder concludes:

> Ended is the Passover Seder
> According to custom, statute, and law.
> As we were worthy to celebrate it this year
> So may we perform it in future years. . . .

The company sings *LShana HaBa-a B'Yershalayim,* "Next Year in Jerusalem."

It takes some hours to complete the seder. One rises from the table, full of soup, fish, chicken, vegetables, a sponge cake, perhaps a compote. There are matzo crumbs to brush off the table and wine stains to bleach out of the white table-cloth.

In Israel the seder is performed once. Elsewhere, it is performed twice. We call our Women's Seder the third seder, and perform it just preceding or following the other two seders. The entire holiday of Passover is eight days.

Searching for Leaven and the Four Questions

IN THE FILM *Miriam's Daughters Now,* Rachel Stein and Maya Pollack, daughters of a painting curator and director/actor, search the studio as the circle of women yell, "Hot! Hotter! You got it!" Applause, as the girls hold up the packet of crumbs.

The search for leaven occurs the night before the first seder. Our feminist seder often precedes the family seder and coincides with the searching and the symbolic burning of the detritus of the year.

The search for leaven is filled with mystery.

I remember my grandmother, kerchief around her head, feather in hand, candle before her, appearing ghostlike at night. The candlelight would flicker across the dresser mirror as she passed silently through my bedroom, on her search throughout the house.

The days of Passover are full of symbols that recreate the time of Exodus. My shelves have been cleared. We have done the big Passover shopping for specially designated foods. All the year-long staples of cereals, crackers, bread, flour are removed. It is more than Spring housecleaning. It is soul-clearing.

I bow to the gathered. We are in the mystery together.

We name the leaven, the *hametz,* the detritus of our lives. At the time of *Miriam's Daughters Now,* in 1984, the women said, "cowardice; pride; self-doubt."

"My high rent," said spirited young Claudia Weinstein.

Bella said, "I suppose I have to name something, some fault, or I'll be thrown out of here. A certitude which some people may regard as opinionated, though I don't."

In the Legacy of the Daughters, in '89, the daughters and

mothers would rid themselves of everything from shyness to physical fears to being cut off from their childhood feelings.

In 1992, we were not so introspective. The walls of the outer world were crashing upon us. We did not name it leaven this time.

We spoke of the blood of the lamb with which the ancient Hebrews marked the lintel of their doors. The Angel of Death would separate the Hebrews from the Egyptians, passing over them on the way to the Slaughter of the Firstborn.

"Women have shed enough blood this year," I say. "Let us write the plagues on the lintel of the doors so that the Angel of Death will pass over and the Angel of Life will come to live with us."

Robin Pogrebin took a magic marker, and wrote on a scroll, rimmed in red. It had been a tough year. There were so many plagues, there were columns of them, a whole portico of plagues, enough to describe a dysfunctional society. They called out:

Silicone Implants
Crown Heights Racial Strife
Agunot **(Jewish women not given religious divorce)**
Battered Women and Children
Death of Supreme Court as a Court of Last Resort (Bella's)
Opening of the Ozone
Death of Women and Children Because of Environment
Unavailability of RU486
TB
Increased Number of Starving People
Cutback in Social Programs
Size of Military Budget
Death Penalty

Homophobia
The Rape Trials of the Accused: Willie Kennedy Smith; Mike Tyson; the Mets; and the St. John's Lacrosse Team and, too often, the victim not receiving justice
Death of Liberalism
Deserting Fathers
Sexual Abuse
Starving Iraqi children
Poverty
George Bush
Clarence Thomas, "Truth Was Murdered" (Bella's)
Strife in (former) Yugoslavia
Women and children with AIDS
Massacre by Hussein
Women with Breast Cancer

By our Seventeenth Seder, there had been a shift. When we first met in 1976, perhaps it was leaven, perhaps something else, but I had asked the gathered: "What promises were not fulfilled?"

Their lives had not been fulfilled: The promise of time, the promise of love, the promise of gainful employment not fulfilled. The promise of respect, the promise of honor, even the false promise of enduring youth, not kept. We did not know as we named our malaise, our disappointments, our realities, that from 1976 to 1992 we did not have the luxury of disaffection. We were entering an era where affection, connection to the life, the world outside of our magic circle was where the new reality lay. That was in political disenfranchisement.

Our most eloquently expressed Four Questions—asked by Daughter, answered by Mother—were written one seder by Michele Landsberg and her daughter Jenny Lewis.

Jenny asks her mother the first question:

1. **Question:** Why is this seder different from all other seders, and why do we still feel the need to create a feminist seder?
   Her mother answers: Because, though it's fifteen years since our rabbis, Phyllis and Esther, created a seder that celebrated the exodus of women, we are still a lost tribe. Men still want to sing solo at the Passover feast, in the Knesset (the Israeli Parliament), in the synagogue, and at the Kotel (the Western Wall). Men still insist on making laws that govern women's wombs. While some men still seek to silence our voices, Miriam's daughters must sing sweeter, bolder, louder.
2. **Question:** But next year in Jerusalem, will there be peace between men and women, equal dignity for Jew and Arab? Will our prophet Miriam be exalted? Will the daughters of Pharaoh's daughter join us in the dance?
   Answer: Our hope and courage spring fresh and green as parsley. But this year and next year we

shall still dip the sweet herbs in salt and angry tears. We will not taste one without the other.

3. **Question:** The Iron Curtain has been torn open, the Berlin Wall tumbled like Jericho. Will those trumpets sound in our homeland, too?

   Answer: Spring comes every year; the sound of the turtle dove is heard in the land. Though many still harden their hearts, though men still hide from women behind the *mechitzah* (religious barrier), our faithful observance of the women's seder reminds us of the power of good and true ideas to break down walls and build a new Jerusalem.

4. **Question:** Why then are we still so few? Why do only a handful of women come together to sing Miriam's song?

   Answer: Many of us still live enslaved to fear and insecurity; many have not left *mitzraiim,* that narrow place; many more have set forth on that journey but still wander in the desert, confused or led astray by ancient bonds of slavery.

   But our history tells us that in every generation, some will rise up against slavish ideas and narrow fears. We seder sisters must be a light to Jewish women. Tonight, this very night, more women celebrate with us at feminist seders in Montreal and Toronto.

**THIS YEAR IN *MITZRAIIM*,
NEXT YEAR IN JERUSALEM!**

Singing the Table of Contents and the Blessings

THE SEDER BEGINS with the singing of the Table of Contents, the Order of the Seder. We, the women, sing a new order. I wrote:

THE ORDER

We bless one another
We wash each other's hands.
We dip greens in saltwater
And wash pain with tears.

We divide matzoth
And hide our past.
We tell Haggadah
And each her own tale.

We bless matzoth
And paths in the sand.
We eat *morror,*
of the bitter past.

We set the table
For the women's supper.
We find the halved matzoth
That's dropped from our lives.

We end with grace,
with blessing and song.
We greet the night
and the following dawn
In the bosom of friends,
The seder of our own.

At this point there is the *kiddush,* the prayer for wine.

In *Miriam's Daughters Now,* Naomi Newman of the Traveling Jewish Theatre sings the candles into flame. Over the years guests have feminized the prayers and I have written new blessings on going into the Passover holiday or blessing the lighting of Sabbath candles, and coming out of Sabbath.

In 1992 Lisa Gerstein, Lilly's "surrogate" daughter, came with new appellations. She had spent 1991 in Jerusalem, studying at Pardes, a religious institute for women.

She passed around a sheet of revised prayers.

"I spoke with the women rabbinical students at Hebrew Union College," she said, as we looked at the new *bruchot,* blessings. "Their spirit is here tonight also."

To whom do we sing?

The Holy One is *Gaol-tanu, ima-ha-olam,* our Redeemer, Mother of the World.

She is *Ha Raham-aima,* Compassionate Giver of Life.

She is *Makor HaHaiim,* Source of Life.

She is our neighborly spirit, the Shekhinah.

The women in Jerusalem still know what to call You Know Who.

Our knowledgeable guests alter familiar phraseology. Mikhal Shiff, a cantorial student then at Hebrew Union College, came to us in 1985 to strengthen our voices.

She took this phrase from the traditional prayer:

> In every generation,
> each man
> is obliged to see himself
> as though
> he went out of Egypt.

Then Mikhal Shiff sang:

> *B'Chol Dor V'Dor*
> *Hayava Isha Lirot*
> *Lirot et Atzma Ki Ilu Hi*
> *Ki Ilu Hi yataz-a mi'mitzrayim*

> In every generation,
> every woman
> is obliged to see herself
> as though she went out from Egypt.

It is still so radical to change the familiar that one's senses are startled.

Each item on the seder list is noted and has its space.

When the candles are lit, one is mesmerized by the flame, for the candle never burns down the same way.

These candle-lighting prayers were written over the years for different seders where a photocopied sheet would be distributed of the business at hand: the Order of the Seder, the participants and their assigned roles, in addition to the group readings. Usually, prayer would be by the group rather than led by an individual acting for the group in the old hierarchy. So, too, the washing the hands, where we wash and dry one another's hands.

We light candles, together:

> Together we spread the light
> within us is more than light
> There is internal glow,
> There is eternal flame.

At our Fifth Seder, 1980, it was *Havdallah,* a Saturday night, the going out of the Sabbath. We removed the white Sabbath cloth. We turned our faces back to the daily.

The twisted *Havdallah* candle was lit, its smoke braiding upward:

> Shekhinah, we sing a new song unto Thee
> with soaring melody,
> in Miriam's memory,
> we sing a new song unto Thee.
>
> *Hallel* for the Deity,
> *Hallel* for the singer,
> with honey on the tongue,
> with gift of song,
> and beads of words,
> we ornament the air for Thee,
> We sing a new song unto Thee.

We prefer to have the "third seder," our seder, on a night other than Friday so that our friends who guard the Sabbath can attend. We have carelessly or conveniently chosen to forget once in a while and missed valuable women.

Here are two more songs of coming out of holiday.

HAVDALLAH

To mark the difference
to separate, to divide, to set apart.
I will trust and not be afraid
with this congregation of women
and the new beginning together.

and

Blessings on the Shekhinah,
the maker of fire.
Let us be aware
of the division
of light and darkness,
of work and rest,
of self and others,
of holiday and daily.

Let us, as daily women,
as well as women of holy days,
know that there is no holiday
without the preparing for it,
nor is there an ordinary day
unless we make the bed for it.
We are both slaves
and free women.

We pass a spice box around and sniff the odiferous going
out of the Sabbath with stick of cinnamon, twig of clove,
hard nut of nutmeg.

DRAMA OF THE SEDER
There are at least three dramatic moments in the seder: lift-
ing aloft the seder plate and pointing out to the assembled
the symbolism of its ingredients; opening the door to the
prophet; and recovering the broken *afikomen,* each of the
guests sharing in the eating of it. In the traditional seder this
happens right after the seder meal. We, of the Feminist
Seder, do not interrupt for the meal, for the likelihood of
our resuming is slight.

By the Third Seder, 1978, we lifted the seder plate for all to see:

"This is the seder plate.

"The plate is flat. Woman is flat, like a plate, flat in the relief of history. Here we give her dimension in our mythic memory. We do not merely act as servers but service one another and make ancient symbols our own."

We named the plate and its objects in the light of our own gender.

"The *Hrain,* bitter herb of our experience, our exclusion.

"The *Haroseth,* the mortar of our lives in these new structures we are attempting to build.

"The *Lamb Shank,* which sets us apart with special markings, which continues the blood imagery of the Haggadah and our own bleeding.

"The *Egg,* that which is our rebirth and which we expel monthly.

"The *Potato* and *Parsley,* for we are earthy, rooted beings.

"*Saltwater* of our tears.

"*Matzoth* of our unleavened hearts."

THE DAUGHTERS' FARE

At the Daughters' Seder in '89, the plate had different fare, such as a key, and the matzoth had a psychological interpretation.

Mychal Springer, then a rabbinical student at Jewish Theological Seminary, reflects on the offering of the seder plate: matzo, *morror,* and the shank bone.

Robin Pogrebin holds up a key.

"This is the symbol for the shank bone. We have the key to our own place. No one is there for us. We have to be there for ourselves."

Nahama Broner is a psychologist, treating institutionalized girls. She holds up the matzo.

"Matzo is the food baked for hasty journey. My patients from the projects come to the hospital with nothing, often not even the clothing on their backs. Unclad they go into their adolescence; they journey into their adulthood. What kind of system are we constructing for these children?"

Nahama has another thought about matzo.

"One eats matzo with the baked lamb to appease God, to make sure not to enrage. That matzo, baked by the sun, is a kind of primitive magic which we ingest, the undoing of harm."

Morror is bitterness, usually represented by horseradish. I remember helping my parents prepare the *morror,* grating the horse radish. We would rush to the sink to wash our eyes from the stingingly sharp juice.

The *morror* of 1989, as conceived by Abigail Pogrebin, was of a different kind.

She holds up a hanger from which little objects or disks are hanging.

"Midol for monthly pain," Abigail points out. "Curler for vanity. TV control for the curse of television. This disk says sixty-nine cents, which is the amount on a dollar that a woman earns, and there is a double medallion with Vice President Dan Quayle on one side and the batterer and child murderer, Joel Steinberg, on the other." Both mean women harm.

"The hanger, of course, is the curse of our pre-legalized abortion days."

The next generation claims and renames.

THE AFIKOMEN

Each year we raise the *afikomen* for all to see.

In our new tradition we speak of the breaking of the matzo as a break, a change, from the old order. We hide the past from ourselves and need to redeem it to create a whole from the broken halves.

In the early days of the Seder, the daughters who redeemed the *afikomen* requested of us, as their reward, that we care for them, for each other, that we make peace, and that we continue connection.

When Abigail and Robin Pogrebin were about thirteen years old, they set the tone. They wished their mother Letty to have strength and to be what she needed to be in her life.

At the Fifth Seder, the daughters demanded that we pay them off with commitments and blessings, and so we put our hands on their heads and, with full hearts, blessed them. And the group made a commitment to them; we would know them and care about them.

It is the custom for the father of the firstborn son of the priestly tribe of Cohane to redeem his son from the Priestly Class. So we buy back our girl children as precious, as gifts in our lives.

In 1979, when I was leading a feminist seder in Hollywood, Naomi Kleinmuntz, the daughter of television writer, Hindi Brooks, demanded that to surrender her stolen *afikomen,* one of us help her plant her garden. One of us, Gelya Frank, an anthropologist, arrived at Naomi's house a few days later and commenced digging.

We have said, at our seders, after we've all shared bits of the matzo, "Next year in Jerusalem or wherever your Jerusalem lies."

The year of the Daughters' Seder, 1989, the *afikomen* was made cosmic and connective as our daughters instructed us in how to be their mothers as well as the mothers of the women's movement.

REGENDERING PASSOVER PRAYERS

We amended the words of the traditional Haggadah, "Thou shalt tell thy sons on that day, 'This is on account of what the Lord did for me that I came out of Egypt.' " Instead, we said, "Thou shalt tell thy daughters on that day, 'This is on account of what the Shekhinah did for me when I came out of Egypt,' for we are not sons but descendants of Righteous Women, the Midwives, Shiphra and Puah, Yocheved, the mother of Moses, and Miriam his sister. We were led forth by the *Rouach,* the Spirit, the Shekhinah."

After the Four Questions, then come the Answers. The traditional Haggadah begins, *Avadim hayenu,* "We were slaves of Pharaoh in Egypt. . . . "

Hebrew is strictly gendered and the language of address, of preference, is masculine.

We, at the women's seders, have said:

> Slaves were we to Pharaoh
> Slaves were we to sorrow
> But we brought ourselves forth
> with our own hand
> and left yesterday for tomorrow.

We knew by now that we had to correct memory and history and myth with new myth, with revision, with data.

THE SENSUAL SEDER

We women at our seder talked about this festival being both one of exodus and one of ecstasy, that in the days of the Temple, *Hag Ha Matzoth,* the Holiday of Matzoth, was celebrated by a pilgrimage to the Temple with the bringing of the Spring harvest. Passover time is that of lambing and harvesting and it is also the week when *Song of Songs* is sung.

"We women," I have said, "are earthy and lunar, of both body and soul, and we must sing of our sensual as well as of our spiritual selves.

"The *haroseth* of apples–nut–wine is also a reminder of the apple orchard, of making love under its fragrant blossoms as the lovers did in *Song of Songs.*"

We want our growing daughters always to be comfortable in their bodies.

THE CUPS OF WINE

It is the custom to drink four cups of wine during a seder. Much of the *Haggadah* is based upon four—the Four Sons, the Four Questions. We use the four *bruchot,* blessings, toasts, to mark the phases of our journey. And the toasts have changed along the way from our first to now.

As published in *Ms.* magazine in April 1977, the four cups of wine are accompanied by these toasts.

> **1) I feel the need to be saved.**
> **2) I want to save myself.**
> **3) From these plagues upon myself, I look for the way of self-redemption.**
> **4) I take the responsibility of becoming a free woman or a free man.**

By 1984, our Ninth Seder, the toasts had changed:

> **1) I begin the journey into my history.**
> **2) I journey with other women.**
> **3) To those on the other shore, not able to risk the plunge.**
> **4) The raising high of women who were laid low.**

In the 1992 revision, redemption did not seem to be the right feeling when women were under such siege everywhere. Journeying forth and going back seemed urgent. The toasts are:

1) **We return to Egypt.**
2) **We return to the desert.**
3) **We drink to the dregs from the cup of knowledge.**
4) **I went to Egypt. I went to the desert. I learned our history. I am still on my journey.**

Our daughters have a different journey than we. Our guests have also journeyed from someplace else. Their markers along the way are shaped by their lives. But always, our gender marks the grammar.

THE STORY

The Telling of the Story is the same, yet different, for there are players upon whom new light is shed in *The Women's Haggadah*. As light is shed upon them, so it is upon us. Our studying changes.

In Lilly's *midrash,* learned lesson, on Miriam in 1987, Lilly spoke of Miriam as a moral force, a caretaker.

Miriam had dictated to the men of her father's generation the appropriate behavior when they all rejected their wives. Miriam told Moses to give up the ascetic ways that were upon him since he had his vision in the desert and to return physically to his wife, Tsiporah. In 1992, Lilly spoke of the midwives, Shiphra and Puah, and the necessity of rebellion.

Phyllis has also spoken of Miriam and the importance of water in contemplating the prophet—the Nile, the well of clear water that followed Miriam in the desert. In 1992 Phyllis spoke of Batya, the daughter of Pharaoh, and the speculation that she herself had been affected by the rearing of Moses, that perhaps she even converted to her son's religion and left with the tribe.

What made the Story different from the traditional readings was the incorporation of self, the insertion of our lives into the tale, to create living history. We spoke of our mothers, our fears, hurts, and hopes. And, thereby, we created a new legend.

PART FOUR

 The Themes

The Righteous and the Veiled

LEGEND IS to collect, gather, or read a story handed down from the past. With the Passover story, it is customary to interrupt for commentary, disputation, and family discussion.

The traditional Passover Haggadah is often amended and made particular or timely. For instance, there is the Nature Haggadah of the kibbutz movement, the Civil Rights Haggadah, the Egalitarian Haggadah, as well as the Ecological and Zen Haggadoth.

There may be as many new conceptions, new illustrations, as the generations that have passed since the Exodus, for each family varies in its telling.

We Seder Sisters bring new themes each year—kabbalistic, political, personal.

Here are the themes around which our seders were organized:

> **The Thirty-Six Righteous Women: Each guest brought the name of a just woman (1978).**
>
> **Veiled References; Woman and the Veil: Iran had become a fundamentalist republic, with the women once again in *chador*. In sympathy, the Seder Sisters veiled themselves (1979).**
>
> **Sayings of the Mothers: Our mothers' wisdom and recipes. New songs for *Havdallah*, the going out of the Sabbath, and psalms of praise and sorrow for our mothers (1980).**
>
> **Human-Sized Miracles: We came with work-a-day stories of our mothers and historical mothers (1981).**
>
> **The Kabbalah of Seven: The mystical number 7 and predictions of the future (1982).**
>
> **The Kabbalah of Eight: The snake with its tail in its mouth, the journeying and returning**

of 8; the introduction of the Sacred Schmata (1983).

Who Are Your Miriams? Tents in the Desert: We each brought the name of a "Miriam," someone who led us across the sea. We become movie stars in Rivlin's film, *Miriam's Daughters Now* (1984).

New Bridges, New Songs, New Commandments: Members of the Black/Jewish dialogue come to the seder. Additions to the Haggadah. Presentation of The New Ten Commandments (1985).

Intra-Group Mediation: Quarreling between us. Paley speaks of quarreling and settling. The family of women is both in pain and soothes that pain (1986).

Loss and Continuity: Death mourned. Children arrive and ask questions (1986).

The Time of Covenant: We are thirteen. Chesler calls us "Daughters of the Mitzvah." We almost destroy the Sacred Schmata (1988).

The Legacy of the Daughters: The daughters plan the seder, ask their questions, bring us to a place we have never been before (1989).

Omission, Absence, Silence: The group discusses the omission of women from history, the silence of women in their past, the absence of women politically and spiritually (1990).

The Plagues We Live Under: Reacting to war, the group is politically split; we speak of plagues, personal and political, that have beset us this past year (1991).

The Change Makers: Those who altered the world in large or modest ways—educators, writers, young journalists—women from seventeen to seventy honored (1992).

The word theme is from Greek, "a proposition." One of the Seder Sisters would propose an idea and we would wind through it, wrapping it around ourselves like a scarf, like our Sacred Schmata.

We would go back to the text each year, read Exodus again and again, for it is the basic story: a baby in a floating basket, rescued by royalty, growing up and identifying with his people, exile, magical signs in the desert, meeting the Ruler of Rulers, returning to his suffering people. Led by the prince, with the Ruler of Rulers above them, they cross the sea and arrive dry-shod. They live in the desert forty years, conquer a people, and establish a nationhood. It is about suffering, redemption, and reward. It is revolutionary.

All people need their history, their mythos.

Women may need it most of all, for we have had so little mention, such a small part in history.

THE JUST

Our first chosen theme was the *Lamed Vovnik,* the Thirty-Six Just, on whose backs the world rests, whose laments God hears, whose tears God counts. In Jewish lore the Just have always been men, the Thirty-Six Just Men.

At least thirty-six women attended that night, each with the name of someone righteous. The names were public and private, from Emma Goldman, Rosa Luxemburg, and Simone Weil to an aunt in the Bronx who managed to feed both family and strangers during the Depression by adding "a little something" to the soup.

Grace Paley, who was not to come to us for another five years, was nominated to the status of *Lamed Vovnik.* We were declaring our women heroes, mystics, and prophets.

Women among us were also nominated. Letty nominated Phyllis Chesler for her books, her battles for women.

Jo Oppenheim, a therapist, remembers the 1978 seder. "One of the young women guests spoke of being raped and was weeping. That was a hard one. Still harder was hearing about the trial."

The young woman guest nominated her mother, present in the circle, as one of the righteous, for, even though they lost the case, she had been there for her.

POLITICAL SEDERS

Taking the Veil

Political events influenced our seders. In 1979 Iran had become a fundamentalist state and the women were required, once again, to take the veil. We chose the veil as a symbol of women being forced outside of society, made invisible. Phyllis Chesler, our group symbolist, brought the veil she had worn as a young bride in Kurdistan. Phyllis led this seder with Rabbi Rebecca Alpert of the Reconstructionist Movement. I was on the West Coast, teaching at UCLA, holding my own conference with a group that included the Susan B. Anthony Coven of witches.

In New York, the group took the veil and felt the effect—entombed, narrowed vision, clumsy walk, and separated one from the other.

At this seder, Bea Kreloff spoke of being in another kind of *chador,* when one is large and thought of as ungainly. Bea was wearing a loose-fitting garment.

Bea said, "This is what fat girls had to wear, what I had to wear. There was nothing then to fit us as we grew up."

Across the room, Gloria Steinem sat in an oversized shirt.

"But now," said Bea, pointing to Gloria's shirt, "they are making clothes for all of us, even me."

At which Gloria took the shirt off her back for Bea.

The seders were not for everyone. Some disapproved of our themes and others used them.

"Some people were self-conscious," said my daughter Sari, "when the veil was passed around for each to put on and tell how she felt. They wouldn't wear the veil. They were too shy to speak. And they won't return."

Helen Yglesias, the novelist, was uncomfortable. This was too C-R for her, too autobiographical and, perhaps, glib. She is hard of hearing, and the *chador* blurred the passionate words uttered by the women and made Helen feel doubly the outsider. Helen would satirize women's spiritual gatherings in her novel *Sweetsir.*

Eve Merriam, the poet and playwright, may she rest in peace, watched and listened intently and, not long after, brought out a production at La Mama Theater, produced by Tom O'Horgan, taking off from the Haggadah and *Dayenu.*

We were grist for everyone's mill.

The Fast of the Just

In 1981 we were entering a new era. When we spoke of plagues Andrea Dorkin said, "Fascism with a smiling face."

It would be a decade of smiling and smiling, and women's lot reducing and reducing.

This was clear in 1982. At the Kabbalah of Seven seder at Chesler's in Brooklyn, we had a guest who sat quietly during the seder but came up after to Gloria Steinem to ask advice and make a request.

She was Sonia Johnson, the Mormon activist for the ERA, who had been excommunicated from the Church for her activism on women's behalf. Sonia had a plan.

Sonia Johnson was about to take strong action during the closing days of the debate on the Equal Rights Amendment in the state legislatures. She and a group of women supporters would go to Springfield, Illinois, and fast the days or weeks necessary to influence the state legislature to reconsider. Illinois was the only northern legislature to reject the ERA. If they did not change their minds, the bill would be lost.

Sonia left with Steinem's blessings. Sonia Johnson would appear in the Springfield state capitol, dressed in white with her sister-fasters, under the banner: WE HUNGER FOR JUSTICE.

I would drive there from Detroit to join her for a few days. Gloria had kept more than her word of support. She had paid for a van to transport the fasting women to and from the state capitol.

I saw the opposition, the supporters of Phyllis Schlafly, unfurl a banner from the highest balcony of the state rotunda: KILL THE WOMEN; BRING BACK THE LADIES. These same people came to jeer the women in white, to slowly unwrap and masticate candy bars before the fasters. Sonia fainted the day I was there and was carried by ambulance to the hospital. Nevertheless, the women never interrupted their fast until the vote. The ERA was lost, but not for want of ardent belief and great effort on its behalf.

Warring Factions

We differ in our politics in 1991. Some of the sisters sign a pro-peace letter to the *New York Times,* and others among us write in support of the Gulf War for the magazine *On the Issues.*

At the pre-planning session, Letty's living room erupts in disagreement.

"Hussein had to be stopped," says Lilly, "and Israel was in mortal danger."

Edith disagrees with Lilly. War is not a solution, she believes. Extend the embargo.

Edith has been marching in New York with the WIMPS, Women Indicting Military Plans and Solutions. One rainy day, marching in the West Village, the group rushes to shelter with their signs, hand-painted by Edith. The colors begin running down the signs and onto the picketers' coats. The group hurries past a playground where a mother and son pack up to depart.

"Can I have one of your leaflets, ladies?" calls the mother.

"Certainly," says Edith.

"What do those ladies want, Mummy?" asks the four-year-old.

"They don't want their children to go to the desert and fight," answers his mother.

"Oh, no!" says the little boy. "They should stay in the playground and play."

So we are split on whether to stay and play or go to the desert.

It is Jenny Lewis, Michele's youngest daughter, who comes up with the topic for the seder.

"Plagues," she says, "Plagues We Live Under or Plagues of the Mind."

That pleases the warriors and peaceniks alike, and we applaud the suggestion.

We address ourselves to Jenny's topic of "The Plagues We Live Under."

Mira Rothenberg, psychologist and clinical director of the Blueberry Treatment Centers, treats autistic and schizophrenic children. She has written movingly about them in *Children with Emerald Eyes* (New York: Dial Press, 1977).

Her plague is the depression that has hit the city and its health workers and its health facilities.

"Blueberry is closed," says Mira. "Where will all those children go? There's even a long waiting list. Where will they go?"

Nowhere.

Susan Sklar Friedman speaks of her life as a young careerist and married person.

"I have a sense of incompleteness," she says. "As a feminist I have been very successful in my career—a man's career, a film editor—and as a Jew. I have gotten married and am starting a family, but I feel that what I am not successful at, I am incomplete in, is in the world of women. All of the women of my generation are so busy juggling careers we have forgotten about each other."

Her mother, the distinguished professor, Kathryn Kish Sklar, and author of *Catherine Beecher, A Study in American Domesticity,* also has a plague coming out of the political climate.

"My plague is personal and public. I teach about American history. I am not going to be able to speak without crying. It is my grief over what I saw as the potential of American history. I came to it over twenty-five years ago full of the most positive hopes for racial equality, for the potential of this society to go further and create a better world for wage earners.

"This packs a double punch because it is my work. The power of the people in this country to transform society and make the world a better place has been so depleted and misused that I wonder whether it can ever be recovered. How can I recover my hope? I can't let my students know that I've lost hope."

Michele Landsberg, sitting next to Kitty, says, "My plague focuses on my deep alienation from my own people and Israel. My own history was structured around the idealism of . . . collective Zionism, but, bit by bit, it is torn apart. It is as though . . . between me and my people is a Red Sea. On the far shore is a dwarfish Moses shouting, screaming, 'Force, Might, Fighting!' . . . I will never be reconciled to the pain of being separated from my people."

Lilly Rivlin says on *V'he Shamda,* that is, the promise made in the Haggadah, on how every year one has risen against us and the Holy One has destroyed him.

Lilly says, "I have seen Israelis here in the States recovering from the weeks of tension of the war. They believe a miracle took place that there were so few injuries from the Scud attacks. It *was* a miracle. Hussein had to be stopped."

Merle Hoffman, reproduction rights activist, editor of *On the Issues,* says, "I am always on the front line."

Her hospital is often under attack by the anti-choice people, Operation Rescue. Her hospital performs birthing and abortion services. The Bishop of Brooklyn arrived with his parishioners and chained himself to a fence. When Merle came out to attempt a dialogue, he called her Hitler!

"I am not afraid of war," says Merle, "nor should Israel be."

As for war, Nahama says that there is a lack of models in the Hebrew Bible for negotiation.

"There is a history of confrontation and war, even with the women heroes. Queen Esther negotiated for the lives of her people but, also, for the death of her enemies. In our religion, in our myths, we do not have a negotiation paradigm," she concludes.

Our anger from the pre-planning has been dissipated by the talking, the reflecting, the stating, and the hearing.

I have spent a week writing poems about my plagues. I distribute copies so we can read together:

THE DISASTERS OF WAR

1. THE PLAGUE OF MOONLIGHT
On the 16th day of January
of the Gregorian calendar,
on the first day of the month of *Shevet,*
of the Jewish calendar,
also *Rosh Hodesh,* the New Moon,
while the synagogues praise the One
who fixed the stars, the sun,
and the moon in place,
the planes take off.
The war commences by sunlight, by moonlight.
The planes glint over sand and city.
The world counts the ends of its calendars.

2. THE PLAGUE OF HOLY PLACES
The holy places of one people
are the Western Wall, the city of David,
the Cave of Machpelah.
The holy places of another people
are the ziggarut of two thousand years,
the minaret of the ninth century,

the walls of Haara, the Arch of Cleisiphon,
the Gates of Ishtar.

On one people missiles fall,
reducing memory to rubble.
On another people, bombs rain,
like the plague of moraine,
the plague of darkness,
the plagues of despoiled water,
the slaughter of sons.

If people are not holy,
are their places sacred?
If holiness is destroyed,
what remains?

3. THE PLAGUE OF SACRIFICE

In the deserts the mothers are watching.
Their shadows are short in the high sun.
They're tombstones, mounds, shrouds.
The mother of Isaac is watching and waiting.
The mother of Ishmael watched her parched son.
There is reprieve
with ram in the thicket
the well of cool water.

Mary watches in the city
skirted by the desert.
There is no reprieve.
Her lap is laden with grief.

This is not the past,
though once, in cultist times,
the priests of the tribe of Levi
sacrificed the bull, the ram, the lamb,
all male without blemish.
The sons of Aaron splashed the blood
on all sides of the altar.
The Temple became an abattoir.
Except for the Sumerians
and their scapegoat,
no one does that now.

Instead we have substituted
human sacrifice.

The mothers of the desert
open their dark robes
to enfold
their sacrificed children.

A year later, on the anniversary of the date when the war commenced, some of the Seder Sisters marched, holding up signs of the great loss of life, of the extent of the pollution. The lead figure in the processional was an Uncle Sam on stilts. A drum sounded a steady beat inside and outside of Grand Central Station on the frigid day of the winter memorial march.

One passerby stopped.

"What is it for?" he asked.

"The Gulf War," he was told.

"Forgotten," he shook his head. "Don't you understand? Gone and forgotten."

Our Mothers and Our Foremothers

WE NAMED ourselves, reconceived our foremothers, and then we were ready to explore our relationships with our mothers.

From the first Women's Seder in 1976 until today we begin by introducing ourselves through our matrilineage.

MATRILINEAGE

When it is my turn, I say, "I am Esther, daughter of Beatrice (Batya), granddaughter of two sisters, Tsivia and Nechama, for whom my daughters, Sari and Nahama, are named. I have two sons, Adam and Jeremy."

Often we don't know our matrilineal descent.

Naomi Wolf has listed, "Naomi, daughter of Deborah, granddaughter of Mrs. Grandma."

Bea says, "I am *Bracha,* which means 'Blessing,' daughter of Celia."

Eve Abzug introduces herself, "Daughter of Bella, daughter of Esther, daughter of Jenny."

Robin Pogrebin says, "I am Robin, daughter of Letty, daughter of Ceil, daughter of Jenny."

Her twin, Abigail, says, "I am Abigail, sister to Robin and ditto to all the rest."

At the seder in 1991, Amy Goodman, a reporter for New York City radio station WBAI, taped us for an eighteen-minute program to be played at Passover. She signed off: "This is Amy Goodman, daughter of Dorothy, granddaughter of Sonia and Gittle, great-granddaughter of Nahama, Gitta, Rivka, great-great-granddaughter of Breindel."

That young woman knew where she came from.

I wrote a song for the mothers, *Perkei Ima'ot,* Sayings of the Mothers, based upon traditional prayer:

These are the sayings of our mothers.
Let us write them on our cuffs.
Let us carve them upon the lintel of our doors.
Let us inscribe them upon our hearts.

THE FOREMOTHERS

It was at that Daughters' Seder that we spoke of the
Foremothers and took on their personas.

Nahama is the prophet Miriam, with reservations.

"How can I be different from Miriam, who lost her power
when she rebelled and, therefore, could not make change?"

Robin Pogrebin is Deborah.

"The power," Robin says, "isn't given. It's assumed. That's
unusual for a woman to be a judge, a warrior. But there is no
inner life to Deborah for her to have had that strength. My
promised land would allow me to be all things, judge and
woman warrior also."

Abigail Pogrebin is Sarai, before she was Sarah, "Wife/sis-
ter of Abraham and in bondage."

Bea inserts, "I can see how Sarah was of an oppressive
mold. We live by that code."

Deborah Wolf says, "I was named by my mother for
Deborah, after years of my mother's trying to conceive. I was
named to be a warrior."

Deborah Wolf, a Ph.D. in anthropology, is now a therapist,
a warrior fighting for her clients, ill with AIDS.

Letty thinks about the character Deborah, who, Letty says,
reminds her of herself.

"Deborah was judgmental. I worry about that in my life.
That is my tendency, to judge."

Bella inserts, "Men created the image of Deborah. She
advised going to war. That's all we know about her. Miriam
is an unclear figure. She fits in as a great sister. There is no
substance as to what she's about."

Gloria has an inspiration. She interrupts Bella.

"Let us explore what would have happened if Deborah
had said no to war, Miriam had said no when sent out of the
tent, Sarah had refused her role."

Bella agrees and says, "I cannot relate to some of these women. We have to analyze them. Why do we, in a feminist seder, take the male image of women?"

Although argumentative and insistent about the role of the matriarchs, Bella is having the time of her life.

She has told me that the seder is the only time when she doesn't have to rush off to another meeting, where she can listen to and meditate on what others are saying, where she herself can speak loudly or softly.

"Abram," says Bella, using the earliest name of the husband of Sarah, "was our great patriarch and also a great victimizer. And Sarah, through Hagar, is the first exponent of surrogacy, of surrogate motherhood. Sarah's whole life was dependent upon what Abram needed."

Gloria is thinking of ancestors who were meaningful to her mother and herself.

"I loved that story of Ruth and Naomi," says Gloria. " 'Wither thou goest, I go,' is what my mother Ruth quoted, and she told me that a woman said this to another woman instead of to a man!"

"And to a mother-in-law yet," laughs Bella.

This night, we either totally accepted or dismissed all of our biblical foremothers.

EMBRACED AND EMBATTLED: MOTHERS AND DAUGHTERS

We had several seders dealing with the embraced and embattled relationship with our mothers. Our seders were like the phases of growing up. We began with anger, condemnation, continued into connection, then to questioning and to praise. Our daughters helped us gain maturity.

I had led a Feminist Seder on the West Coast in 1979 and brought some of this material to the New York seders that dealt with the theme of mother and daughter.

I said in California in 1979, "It is unacceptable for our mothers to be the mapmakers of their daughters' lives, the wardens, warners of harm, the terrifiers of their daughters.

"Some of us have had to mother our mothers.

"Some of us who are mothers have been suckled dry by our children.

"Some of us who are mothers are now colicky and in need of being held also. . . .

"We commemorate our mothers, for better or worse, richer or poorer, in sickness and in health, for we are wedded to them."

The following year, 1980, the seder's theme was Sayings of Our Mothers, their words and their recipes. Lilly read her mother Bella's recipes.

I brought a poster quoting from the Yiddish poet of the early twentieth century, Kadia Molodowsky: "Sometimes in the night, the women of our family will come to me in dreams."

So we spoke of snapshots of women who came to us in dreams of the night, the mother lode that gleams upon us.

An adult education writing class in San Francisco made that poster, surrounding Molodowsky's words with photos of their own families: immigrant grandmothers in babushkas, their mothers in 1940s hats and dark lipstick, themselves as children.

We began to think of ourselves as posters, our lives as a photographic collage.

We spoke of our mothers, of how we hurt one another and how to heal one another.

I wrote songs of praise and sorrow.

O, my mother who labored
and birthed her life and mine
And she oppressed herself
and named herself her own Egyptian.
She was her own taskmaster,
afflicted with burden.

And she cried out
but none of us heard,
for the kitchen water was running,
the washing machine was changing cycles.

She cried out
and none of us heard her groaning.
Now, in memory, I hear.

My mother, whose exile was in her own home.
My mother, who wrung out sheets with her strong
hands.
My mother, who nourished us with food and
laughter
but preferred her sons to her daughters.

O, my mother
who would not regard herself as matriarch
of this tribe, this pride of women.

We were asked to speak about madness and forgiveness.

Restorative Prayers for Mad Mothers

Mothers, in the unmarked wilderness
Mother, who crossed the reed-filled sea,
we beat our drums to lead you in steady beat.
We sound the ram's horn
to guide your return.
We sing songs of praise
to continue your days.

Mothers, live through madness
live through the heat
of desert sun upon your head,
of time of desolation.
We, your daughters, are here,
your oasis, your reader and singer,
accompanist and archivist,
the teller of your tale.
Mothers, return to us
and to the banks of sanity.

That was the only time we spoke so mournfully of our
mothers.

One woman who had joined us at the Third Seder, 1979, and for many years thereafter, was Dr. Lilly Engler, a psychiatrist. She had a refugee tale to tell.

She described how, as a young girl, she had put together a boat and paddled it down the Danube, rescuing her mother and herself. No one had yet spoken of rescuing a mother.

Michele, some years later, would talk about her mother.

"My mother," said Michele, "had a capacity for radiant joy in small, beautiful things. I learned from Mother to love the gifts of women who are different from me. You reconcile these different poles by living. I taught my mother, finally, to love and approve of me."

At the seder Miracles in the Hand, 1981, Ruth Kroll of the Detroit Women's Forum read from her mother's memoir about coming to the States from Russia as a young woman, of the deaths she witnessed when so young and on her own. The voice was nonliterary, but the memoir dealt with the daily heroic.

Jane Dobija, also from Detroit, and later reporting for National Public Radio as their correspondent from Warsaw, played tapes of Detroit women from Hamtramck, a Polish enclave in the city. These factory workers, elderly women now, had made "human-size" miracles, changes in their working conditions. The women spoke about their organizing a union at R. J. Donn Cigars in the thirties, demanding higher pay and better working conditions. They recalled that their husbands brought them their babies to nurse as the days of the sit-down passed into weeks.

They were our historic mothers also, ordinary women whom circumstances made extraordinary. Their miracles were work a day.

We also gave ourselves, at that seder, permission to be disobedient daughters.

Seder means order, and in terms of tradition we were disorderly. We sat around a set tablecloth. The *Shulchan Aruch,* the Set Table, is a book of precepts from our sages. But we disobedient daughters upset the table, unsettled the assumptions of the past.

In 1984 we proclaimed our mothers and called them Miriam. Or we spoke of mother-mentors, as we had in that First Seder. I quoted from the song "Who Knows One," sung every Passover. It is a counting song. For nine we sang, "Nine are the months of childbirth."

"This year," I said, "*Tesha Anee Yodaat*. I know nine. Nine are the months of childbirth. We are all daughters, having lain inside of our mothers those nine months. Some of us have chosen to be mothers and have had our own lying-in, and all of us have chosen to be friends and to come together in celebration."

When we spoke of our Miriams, the painter Audrey Flack told about the women she met when her child was young and was discovered to be autistic.

"The fathers of the children had left," she said. "It was too much for them. It was too much for the mothers also but they stayed. Some of the women drank. But they stayed."

How brave they were, often deserted and alone with their child who was both their love and their burden.

"I want to put those women here, right in the center of the table, my Miriams."

This was the seder where Eve Abzug turned to Bella and called her Miriam.

We were determined to be Miriams in our lives.

Grown-Up Mothers, Grown-Up Daughters

IN 1988 Lilly Rivlin suggested that the daughters put on the next seder. We approved, I thought, unanimously. Phyllis was quiet. It seems she was hesitant. As the seder neared, she phoned the daughter-planners to tell them that she would not attend. She felt she was being punished for being the mother of a son. A pall was cast. Our symbolist, our expressive presence would be absent.

Nevertheless, as we gathered at the uptown apartment of Robin and Abigail Pogrebin, Phyllis and her chosen daughter were there.

THE GENERATIONS

The daughters sat in the place of honor as leaders of the service.

Robin Pogrebin began, "This is an exchange, a dialogue. We want to proceed independently and together, mother and daughter. You are our teachers, builders, spokeswomen. Now there is transference and inheritance."

Naomi Wolf said, "This is the passing on. The daughters will question; the mothers will answer; and we will create together a legacy of the seder."

Nahama added, "Our questions and the mothers' articulation of our legacy will move into making the whole."

The daughters had composed new questions for their mothers:

"Why are our mothers not more supportive of their daughters?"

"Where are our mothers? Where are you? Why don't you come to us?"

One, Alexandra Stein, sixteen, Gloria's surrogate daughter, asked, "When does it get easier? Does it?"

Maria Goldberg asked, "How do you keep the concern of both generations and make a bridge?"

Tamar Haut, Phyllis's choice to attend the seder, sat shyly, huddled into the knees of her blue jeans.

She asked, "How do we stop being a daughter and still be a daughter?"

Eve Abzug, Bella's daughter, is at her first woman's seder.

"How do we fully pass on the legacy given us?" she wants to know.

Mychal Springer, one of the planners of this event, asks about the relationship between the child and the adult: "Does one still have to live in that tension?"

Alexandra Stein looks at us and says, "My mother died when I was young, ten, so I gave her the features of all of our women leaders."

We, who look nothing alike—from Phyllis's full lips and dark hair to Bea's straight hair to Edith's curly gray hair to my Mediterranean hair to Letty's and Gloria's straight blond hair—wonder about this composite mother.

Naomi Wolf says, "It has been hard for the daughters because you are strong, such powerful women. It is scary! We are the second-generation immigrants in the women's movement."

Her mother, Deborah, is seated behind Naomi and smiles at her daughter's intelligence. Deborah was a classmate of Lilly's at UC Berkeley in the sixties and, with her daughter Naomi, has attended several of our seders.

Abigail says, "You've thrown and we have grabbed. The broken *afikomen,* the matzo, is whole, for you have answered our questions."

HAMETZ

When we introduced ourselves by our matrilineage at the beginning of the seder, we were also required to tell of the *hametz* of which we wished to rid ourselves, that which burdened our journey and prevented our making Exodus.

Gloria said, "I am Gloria, the daughter of Ruth, who is

the daughter of Ruth. My *hametz* is still being cut off from my childhood."

Tamar Haut is nineteen, big-eyed and shy. When it comes time for her to introduce herself and tell her *hametz,* what leaven she would give up, she whispers, "My shyness."

Robin, daughter of Letty, wishes to unburden herself of Pressure; Lilly Rivlin of Despair; Letty of Physical Fear (which surprises those of us who have seen her in traffic on her motorcycle).

Bea "wishes to unburden us all of AIDS."

Pan and Dora, friends of the Pogrebin girls, wish to rid themselves respectively of "an inability to forgive" and "lack of love and a self-righteousness."

Michele, who has rushed in from Canada for the seder, would unburden herself of "self-destructive actions left over from destructive feminine self-accusation."

Eve Abzug wishes to unburden herself of "that remnant of fear which keeps me from making a leap of faith."

Bella smiles at her youngest daughter. She would burden herself with her daughter's *hametz*.

Bella would unburden herself of "that intolerance of people who don't meet the standards of philosophy which I believe, and my anger at failure on the part of myself, but, more often, on the part of others."

THE DESERT

Miriam and the tribe were in the desert. Gloria says, "We are not able to get out of the desert because we are never really in it. How do you get out of one reality into another? We have to go into the desert to retrieve the wild part of ourselves."

Nahama says, "The desert was something different for Miriam than for me. For her it was in exile from community. She was sent to a place, punished by law. When I lived in Jerusalem, I went into the desert to find my own law, to make inner peace. The desert was a place of punishment for Miriam and solace and solitude for me."

Bea remembers another kind of desert, a barren life.

"My whole life was one of denial. I used to think the women were so dumb. I'm going to be different. It turned out I wasn't so different.

"I spent a lot of time," says Bea, "in depression."

We had never thought of her, in our history together, as being a depressive.

"I thought I could break the mold," says Bea.

She couldn't then. She did later.

THE PLAGUES

Letty speaks of plagues. She is politically active against plagues.

"First," she says, "the plagues of poor women alone in their houses, the idea of their being alone with no resources. Secondly, being told what we need, like the 'Mommy Track,' and that plague still plagues us constantly."

She pauses. She thinks of our various contentious years, of our loving yet also endangered community. In an interview with me she has insisted that we are not community, only a single-issue gathering. But still, as she looks around the seder room, there is communal memory.

"Thirdly, I want to speak of a plague among the feminists, *Leshon HaRa,* the evil tongue. Women have got to look into their souls and ask why we speak cruel things. We have to try to live in our sister's skin."

Gloria has a series of plagues to enumerate. She adds one to Letty's.

"One, I hope we can stop killing each other with our words."

Gloria knows this better than anyone. As our longtime, visible leader, the forked tongue flicked out first at her.

"Secondly," says Gloria, "almost all of our plagues are derived from not putting our center into ourselves; putting it into other people."

Bella straightens up at this.

"Thirdly," says Gloria, "our history is a plague, lost and found and lost, without continuity. Fourthly, there is a plague of books like *Men Who Hate Women and the Women Who Love Them.*"

At this point, Bella speaks in a voice so soft we can hardly hear her. She has to clear it once or twice before she proceeds.

She addresses herself to the plague of lack of self-knowledge.

"Nothing can happen," says Bella, "unless there is a funda-
mental sense of self. The sense of self is the most important
guiding point. A sense of love for others may not be a sense
of love for oneself. Many people who engage in social projects often love others but not themselves. The reason we
have not been able to achieve peace is a failure of love."

Her voice is whispery.

"I don't know if I found that love successfully in myself.
And, if you love someone, sometimes you can't express it
fully until it's too late."

In her apartment, on every end table, are photos of Martin,
in his World War II soldier's uniform, or Martin and Bella
as a handsome young couple with their young daughters.
Martin is on all the furniture and still inhabits the room.

The plague of having no center is spoken of again by
Gloria. She re-enters the discourse.

Gloria's hair is pale against her dark, loosely belted blouse.

"I do not want to pass on to any daughter a feeling of having no center. I still have a hard time with that and an inability to get angry."

We all feel, like deep sunburn, the effect of the plague-
ridden past.

ADVICE TO THE DAUGHTERS

"My strongest emotion," says Phyllis, "is tenderness, shoul-
der-to-shoulder women connected. We must try to feel tenderness, all of us.

"Sisterhood is what we have to struggle for," says Phyllis.
"She, Sisterhood, is just a baby. If we don't succeed, we keep
trying. We have to institutionalize that vision called
Sisterhood."

Gloria has advice, earthy advice. It's like new commandments again:

"Trust in the wisdom of everybody.

"There is no hierarchy.

"We can learn from everyone.

"Trust your own wisdom.

"Follow your joy."

We think of having samplers, bumper stickers, posters
made of these words of Gloria, *Perkei Gloria*.

Gloria has more to teach us. She leans over her surrogate daughter, Alexandra Stein.

"Alexandra," she says, "as a spiritual daughter who lost your mother when you were a little girl, you were like me. I lost a mother who was there but lost herself. I learned that men could be loving and nurturing, as your father was, as my father was.

"It has made me much closer to other women because I kept looking for my mother in other women. Until now, I only knew how to be a sister. Because of what happened to my mother, I didn't know how to be a mother until tonight. I wanted a mother so much, I couldn't even admit it. I couldn't hug an older woman. I thought I would dissolve.

"Tonight," says Gloria, "I have learned that I can be mothered by daughters and that solves everything."

It is time for raunchy, bouncy, eloquent Michele. She wears a loose gray jacket with her shirt collar showing. She has a different message.

"Daughters," says Michele, "it is time for some fire and brimstone!"

That makes us sit up.

"I want to speak with the analytical mind of the outsider."

We are startled. She has been with us for three years and seems to have always been our comrade.

"I want my daughters to kindle and flame and know, in their bones, that the opposite of activism is passivity."

Michele continues, "Daughters, I want you to have the courage to cry and laugh and care with inappropriate extravagance. I want you to work for the right life rather than for the good life."

Michele concludes, "Daughters, I want politics to be *Halacha,* the orthodox path, and Sisterhood to be *Derech HaEretz,* the Road to the Holy Land."

That is our new Zionism.

Letty is having *nahas,* pleasure, from her own and our collective daughters. She looks at the young women. Abigail is wearing a light spring dress. Robin, who has had to spend the early part of Sunday reporting for the *New York Times,* has pulled her brown hair back, her hands folded over her raised knees, as she heeds her mother.

"When I was young," says Letty, "no older woman could tell me anything. Now, between what the daughters have seen and what the mothers feel is worth holding on to, there will be a synthesis."

Out comes the Sacred Schmata, the schlocky material Chesler has used to bind us together since our Eighth Seder.

The schmata goes loosely around our daughters, encircling the rabbinical student Mychal with her shoulder-length dark-brown hair, her heart-shaped face, her sweet smile; around Naomi Wolf's waist; caught in the curly hair of Nahama Broner; around Abigail Pogrebin, Tamar Haut, Robin Pogrebin. Some have it wrapped around their wrists. Some of us never want to rewind it and return it to the bag at Letty's side.

Two weeks later, each of the Seder Daughters receives a letter of congratulations and love, signed, "Your Mother, Phyllis."

We never stopped talking of our mothers. Their names resound, mother, grandmother, all the way back, as far back as memory reaches. They hover over and bless each seder.

The Women and Kabbalah

WE HAD SEVERAL kabbalistic seders, where we made reference to numbers and their meaning.

FIVE: A HANDSBREADTH

The Sayings of Our Mothers, 1980, was the Fifth Seder. Five is a sacred number. *Fist* is from five, *finger, foist* also. There is a fist of women on this Fifth Seder.

Everyone brought their fives, like the Five Civilized Indian Nations (Cherokee, Chickasaw, Choctaw, Creek, Seminole), forced to leave their lands.

"This is not so different from the history of women," Chesler reminds us.

Women were deprived of our ceremonial mantle, of the psalms sung to us, the honor paid us. Women went on the reservation.

A hand was extended. Someone's—could it have been Kate Millett's, who started this second phase of the women's movement with her literary critique, *Sexual Politics,* in 1970? Or Kathryn Kish Sklar's, biographer of *Catherine Beecher Stowe* and distinguished professor? A stretched-out hand was a handsbreadth of measurement. We were always finding ways to measure ourselves.

A finger pointed. We were each held responsible, accountable for ourselves and the continuation of our history and community.

SEVEN: THE PAST AND DIVINING THE FUTURE

The Seventh Seder, 1982, was rich kabbalistically. For others, it was the beginning of a time of wearying.

Gloria said, "It was at Chesler's that I learned how I belonged and also did not belong. It was the beginning of less depth. It was more externalized."

Actually, there was a rich outpouring of scholarship and meditation for the Seventh Seder, the Kabbalah of Seven.

Lilly Rivlin had prepared a fine *midrash:*

> " 'All sevens are beloved,' " says the *midrash.* . . . In a
> talmudic prescription to cure a . . . fever: 'Take
> seven door sockets, seven pieces of pitch from seven
> ships, seven handfuls of cumin, and seven hairs from
> the beard of an old dog, and tie them to the neck-
> hole of the shirt with a white twisted cord.' "
>
> The Jubilee Year in Judaism takes place at the end
> of seven sabbatical cycles. . . . At that time the land
> must be allowed to go fallow, the slaves are emanci-
> pated, there is remission of debts. . . .
>
> Seven reigns supreme. The Seven Seas; once it
> was thought there were seven planets; Seven
> Wonders of the World. It took seven days to create
> the world; there are seven days of mourning; seven
> deadly sins. So what does it mean?
>
> *Sheva*—seven—the root of *sheva* also means "to
> take an oath, to swear," *nishba,* to do something
> seven times. A righteous person falls seven times
> and rises again. . . .
>
> Which brings me to the next observation. . . .
> Our daughters are not with us. Have we failed our
> daughters? . . . Have we failed to speak to them in a
> voice they can hear? . . .
>
> Or . . . this is the natural consequence of all fami-
> lies. In seven years we formed a family of women
> and now the daughters are leaving home . . . to be
> pioneers in their own space.
>
> In the first seven years we built with hope. . . .
> They were the full years, and now we come to the
> lean years. . . . We have to protect what we have
> won . . . and let go of those things that want to go
> their way.

We were to address ourselves to the presence or absence of
our daughters over and over. They were our continuity and
yet they, like us, took their own path. The idea of family, the
disappointment when we did not act in a familial fashion,
absorbed us and our energy as the years passed.

We were welcomed to Chesler's Brooklyn brownstone

home. Her four-year-old son, Ariel, and his friend tiptoed around the edges of the tablecloth set on the floor or rushed up and down the stairs in their excitement. They were the first males at our seders.

We would see Ariel again in five years.

Chesler had prepared a twelve-page booklet for us, filled with scholarly and fanciful notations. We learned that the number seven is the most sacred number of all. She quoted Helen Blavatsky, in *Isis Unveiled,* on mystical meanings of seven:

> The number seven reappears on almost every page of Genesis. . . . We find it conspicuous in the Book of Job. . . . This number . . . again appeared in Christianity with its
> seven sacraments
> seven capital sins
> seven virtues (four cardinal and three theological) [(Blavatsky lists)]
> the seven prismatic colors of the rainbow . . .
> the seven labors of magic
> the seven upper spheres
> the seven notes of the music scales . . .
> the seven ages.

Phyllis then reads her own words: "This is a miracle, that we should be alive at the same moment, in full consciousness, painful and jubilant . . . speaking of truth and freedom. . . ."

Phyllis reads next from Genesis of Pharaoh's dream of seven fat cows, the seven lean cows, and of the seven fat ears of corn, followed by the seven lean ears of corn. She speaks of Joseph's dream interpretation of the seven fat years followed by the seven lean years.

Phyllis is also a dream interpreter:

> Washington has declared war on women. . . . They seek to take away our right to abortion, our right to health care. . . . They deny us employment. . . .
> Women in the last years . . . have fallen into a dreadful slump . . . stunned by the swiftness and severity of the war against us. . . .

My sisters: we are in a period of seven lean years. . . . I don't want to prophesy falsely. . . . Did we not prepare well for the famine to come, even though we dreamt it, feared it, spoke of it?. . .

We must harvest our corn. We must store up against famine. We must share it; we must hand it out. Corn is our daughter. Corn is our daughter-self. Corn tells us that we will rise again. . . .

Chesler then distributes the ears of corn, which are not only biblical in reference but also come from the early civilization where the Earth Mother, Demeter, is always shown with ears of corn.

As noted before, Phyllis proves to be no false prophet, as she feared. In 1982 her words would predict the next decade.

We, at this Kabbalah of Seven, recalling the past, prophesying the future, also spoke of the six days that pass and the Sabbath candle lit on the seventh. We lit many candles that night that illuminated ourselves and our thoughts.

We went around the twenty-five women, each speaking of her seven. We did mystical computations, the numbers and letters of our names. We spoke of the seven years past, of seven we named our foremothers.

We blew out candles for those women extinguished in the past year. We opened the door for Miriam and for other women whose presence we needed.

NUMBER EIGHT: JOURNEYING

The figure 8 was our image in 1983: circuitous routes, going and returning, the dragon with its tail in its mouth.

Two who symbolized this number were Marcia Freedman and her daughter Jenny, who had performed and observed the first Women's Seder in Haifa. They were returning to us, journeying from beginning to now.

Lilly read her meditation on eight:

888. Infinity. A line flows forever. 8, one circle. A line flows forever. 8, one circle reflecting another circle . . . the symbol of the Eternal Spirit . . . boundless space. . . .

In tarot, eight estabishes order in memory and

brings it forth, for eight is the time to manifest consciousness.

At the age of eight a child's eyes stop growing. . . .

In our eighth year as a community, we made
conscious our Judaism within the feminist movement. . . .

In our eighth year many of us begin to think of
continuity. I'm so glad to see Naomi (Wolf), Liz
(Abzug), Jenny (Freedman), Nahama (Broner), our
daughters. . . .

In our eighth year we now accept our diversity,
our differences, and acknowledge our interde-
pendence.

An imaginative eight was delivered by Lucille Goodman,
professor of voice at Brooklyn College. Lucille spoke of the
last annual meeting of women musicians and composers,
where it was decided that they, the musicians, controlled
time. They resolved that there be an eighth day of the week
set aside for themselves alone to make music and that eighth
day could come in the middle of the week or the beginning
of the week, but that time was to be declared one's own.

Departure and a kind of returning were implicit in the
remarks of a seder guest, the distinguished filmmaker Mira
Hammermesh.

It began in Poland, where Mira was an intelligent and
rebellious young girl during the impending German invasion. Mira warned her mother that danger was coming.

Mira said to her mother, "I will not wait here for disaster."

The mother pleaded with Mira to stay. It was too dangerous out there for a young girl. Everything would be settled.
The family must remain together.

Mira was impatient. Reluctantly, the mother told Mira's
older brother to accompany his sister.

Mira turned to look back at her mother for the last time.

"If I had been a better daughter," said Mira, "I would
either be dead or my mother alive."

(Mira has since released a documentary of searching for the
graves of her parents who died in the Holocaust, one at
Auschwitz, the other in the Warsaw ghetto. The movie is

called *Loving the Dead*. When, previously, Mira won the most prestigious documentary prize in Great Britain for her film set in South Africa, *Maids and Madams,* an intimate view of apartheid, she rose to accept the award and said, "This is for you, Mama.")

I quoted to the sedergoers from the study *Women Surviving the Holocaust,* edited by Esther Katz and Joan Miriam Ringelheim (New York: Institute for Research in History, 1983).

An anonymous woman speaks:

> The last Passover, 1942, in hiding, not a crumb of leaven or unleaven; no manna fell from heaven; no water sprung out of the well; no potatoes in the frozen ground. We munched potato peels. We didn't dare to sing. Or to open the door for Elijah.

We wondered how to be such good daughters that we could save our mothers without destroying ourselves.

NUMBER ELEVEN: ADOLESCENCE

The Eleventh was our seder attempting mediation within the group.

I said, "It took two trips to Israel to complete *The Women's Haggadah,* and it has taken eleven performances of it with members of this group, and it is still incomplete. In the tradition of seders, it is added to every year to fit our questions and needs.

"Eleven years later we are coming upon another phase of our meetings. Eleven is an awkward time. We are 'at elevenses,' that is, long-legged, knobby-kneed adolescents. . . .

This year, we must ask ourselves, out of our own experience of harsh words, quarreling, separating, how do women settle conflict among themselves? What is our model, or is it up to us to create new ones? What is justice? As we reshaped the Haggadah to make our history, how can justice include our longings?"

NUMBER TWELVE: MAGIC

At our Twelfth Seder, at the Canadian Mission where Steven Lewis and Michele Landsberg were in residence, we spoke of Twelve.

I said, "*Twelve* is *twine, twin, twilight.* It is also *betwixt and between.* And such a time is right to discuss loss and continuity."

We said that twelve is magical to every group: the twelfth night after Christmas of merrymaking; the twelfth day—the seventh of January—Epiphany; twelve tribes; twelve apostles; twelve labors of Hercules; twelve signs of the zodiac; twelve jurors.

Despite all our kabbalistic conjurings, were we closer to magic, to insight, to merrymaking? Were we more judicious? Under the signs of the zodiac were we more insightful?

With the spread candelabra of seven, the figure-skating 8, were we closer to truth?

▓ Quarreling and Mediating

WE WERE at our most quarrelsome twice, in 1986 and 1988.

Nineteen eighty-six was the year of the big speak-out, organized by Phyllis Chesler and the New York chapter of NOW, on women losing custody of their children. The speak-out was timed for the publication of Chesler's book, *Mothers on Trial* (New York: McGraw-Hill, 1986).

Mothers had flown in for this conference, held at John Jay College. Phyllis was being threatened by men's rights groups who picketed the college and shouted abuse at the participants.

Why had the women lost custody? For a variety of reasons, but for the same reason, as it turned out.

Christina Salk lost custody to the psychologist Lee Salk because, as the judge ruled, he was the one with the higher education who would provide the stimulation. She was merely the homemaker who raised the children while he was getting educated. She was scarcely to see them for ten years.

Another, a woman who had been born and educated in India, arrived here, became an American citizen, and began a career of public service. She was elected mayor of her town in New Jersey. She found her husband moody, militaristic, and peculiar, and sued for divorce. He began taking their son to gun practice and to indoctrination at Lyndon LaRouche's group. She sued for custody. The father was awarded custody. The judge told the mayor that she, holding such a high position in the town, only made the man feel the smaller, and, therefore, he would not take the child from him as well.

Yet a different woman, a psychiatrist from Sweden, lost custody. She was intellectually stimulating. She was responsible. But her husband, also a psychiatrist, should not have to compete professionally as well as in his own home.

Another woman was veiled, fearful of being recognized and being beaten again.

Michele Landsberg, who covered the conference, had chapped cheeks from weeping. Bella Abzug, who sat across the table from me, could be heard sighing heavily.

The women lost custody for being homebound and culturally inferior; for going out of the house to work and, therefore, neglecting the children; for being heterosexual and active; for being lesbian and, therefore, dangerous to the children. The women lost because they were women.

Perhaps it was the arranging of such an ambitious event or hearing the poignant stories told over and over or having had some of the women as her patients that exhausted Chesler. Or needing protection.

Maybe when we do something very large, we have to do something very small to compensate.

Lilly Rivlin was the object of the rage because she did not attend the speak-out. On that day she was busy editing *Miriam's Daughters Now,* which had been invited to an international Jewish film festival in the Netherlands.

Sometimes we can't stop our rage. Even roaring does not make the throat go hoarse. Anger builds on anger.

It was a bad year and a hard seder.

Letty began the seder, "Let this session be about Intra-Group Mediation."

We prepared ourselves to speak on alternative modes of behavior, on ways to communicate.

We reflected that maybe the group had become too important. Maybe we expected too much from it. It could not, after all, cure the pain of childhood, provide sustenance for past neglect.

You would think we had nothing to do but suffer from covetousness, from jealousy. Was this a New York trait? Was this the serpent within the community of women?

Here we were doing this large act of transformation and often had not changed ourselves sufficently. We were still carrying *hametz* into holiday.

Lilly sent a letter to all of us, dated March 31, 1986.

> These are some notes based on discussions with Letty and Esther. Letty suggested we have an activist agenda this year.
>
> The concept is conflict resolution among

women. It opens up the question: Are Women Different? Can we find a way of resolving conflicts that (a) is different from men? (b) resolves conflicts?

How can we settle conflicts?

Sources: (1) Check out Jewish Law

(2) Find a scholar who can discuss precedent and teach by example. . . .

Conflict resolution material, negotiation, and arbitration.

Some thoughts:

Can we forge a new model for conflict resolution? Can we make anger constructive?

Purpose: To create something that can be passed on or passed around, perhaps a document or a model *Beth Din* [rabbinical court of justice]. . . .

There was a mask maker at that seder, Susan Benton, who put on a mask that could, one way, be Sarah, the other, Hagar. We were like that ourselves—two parts of one thing, the legend and its opposite.

Twice Hagar had been sent into the desert weeping by Sarah. Sarah endangered not only Hagar but Hagar and Abraham's son, Ishmael. In the end, the son of Sarah was also threatened with sacrifice. Each woman was to be the mother of great nations.

Lilly said to me, "I remember that seder, you being in the middle between Phyllis and me. You were funny. Kiss to one side. To the other. Mmm! Mmm! *Mamale, bubale.* I was very aware you were dividing your attention."

Lilly said there were two parts to this seder: *maalot,* good parts, virtues, and *hesen henonot,* bad parts, lackings, vices. For her, that seder in 1986 consisted of both parts.

◆　◆　◆　◆

How could we, at this awkward age in our community, turn adolescence into community?

Grace Paley spoke and later recapitulated her remarks for me.

"I lived in an extended household. It was wonderful for a child but hell for adults. There was not only the communism/socialism disagreement but whole family fights, fierce fights we had.

"I really loved every one of them, and each one loved me as the youngest child. I think a lot about all the rage and fury and how hard it was to see people, every one of whom was very special to me, and they never interfered with each other's feelings towards me. I was always on the side of whoever was speaking. It felt to me that they each had some piece of justice. Quarrels were embedded in decades before I was born and things I didn't know about for twenty years.

"My father worked like a horse, tried not to notice anything and support everybody. And my grandmother, a noble woman, was part of this household.

"That is why it was impossible to hold grudges because those angers came from so long ago. It hasn't been something that made me more able to take a position, as you well know, but I haven't been personal and have been able to accept apologies with no trouble," Grace concludes.

Lilly Rivlin, at her turn, said softly, "You are my family. I want to be part of this family. I have no other such family. I do not want to be outside of this community."

Phyllis Chesler was sitting silently, a stone clutched in her hand.

"This is what your heart has become, my sisters," she said.

She spoke of pain and betrayal, as the stone was passed from palm to palm.

"How do we mediate between ourselves?" I ask.

This was my first attempt at feminist etiquette.

"We should remember:

"There should not be anger like a Japanese paper flower that expands in moisture. Anger must be specific.

"Rather than exile or the final insult or, even, excommunication, let there be communication.

"We must move beyond anger to an understanding of self and the other.

"The other is not the opposite, the opponent, but, in a way, another part of the self.

"We must circumscribe the written word, soften the voice. The name called in anger still buzzes after reconciliation.

"There should be a formality of address to the other person, the opponent, until or if there is a coming together. The informal leaves things too loose.

I ended: "Remember that it is in the Jewish tradition to seek peaceful ways out of dispute."

This was probably not the conflict-resolution meeting that Lilly had in mind. But seders are metaphoric and the speaking is elegiac and social methodologies did not seem appropriate.

But we would need to remember. There was another meeting, in only two years, the same issues arising, and maybe and maybe not a healing.

The Strategy of Healing

IN 1988 we were called to the apartment of Lilly Rivlin in
Westbeth.

Her large windows overlooked the Hudson. As Lilly con-
sulted her notes, we watched the sunset over the river.

It was on that pier that, for seven years, Lilly and I con-
ducted the ceremony, "New Year on the Pier," emptying our
pockets of detritus over the Hudson.

Lilly's apartment was steamy from the simmering pot of
thick soup.

Lilly said, "First, have apples and honey," which are always
the blessing for a sweet year.

We dipped the slices into the thick honey and licked our
fingers with the apples.

"Now," said Lilly, "Healing and Strategy. I want to tell you
about the events of the past years. Letty and I have been
working for the Empowerment of Jewish Women
Conference in Jerusalem to be held in December. Our committee, in the American Jewish Congress, has worked hard.
We want to establish a Jewish feminist network. . . . It was
difficult."

Letty said, "Lilly should be applauded, for her job was the
most difficult, as program chair."

Lilly then read us her remarks on what she deemed unacceptable behavior from her seder sisters.

This is her Healing Ceremony, where first she feeds us and
then bawls us out. The remarks are addressed to me but,
more particularly, to Phyllis.

Lilly meant to honor us from the seder group by inviting
some of us to speak at the conference.

Phyllis is funded but nervous about her role as well as her
time slot for speaking. She does not want to compete with
clacking silverware at lunch. Should she go or not? On what

panel will she be scheduled? She will need her own room as she is an insomniac.

I have not yet been funded, so my sin is in postponing acceptance, though I am scheduled for the one panel open to the public. It is only at the last minute that a Canadian film company funds me, to be interviewed in Jerusalem for the film *Half the Kingdom*.

One of us in this group is too present; one is too absent. Lilly commences to read and to teach:

"Whether we like it or not, we are a model for others. If we can't work out conflicts, who can?

"If we can't have peace among the peacemakers, what hope is there?"

Lilly tells us the order of procedure:

1) Each person will have an opportunity to express herself.

2) There will be a review of events: speaking about the conference.

3) We call ourselves the Seder Sisters, but I have not felt sisterly feelings in the last two months. There has been backbiting, demands, anger, and I am ashamed. I feel we have turned the concept of Seder Sister into a sham.

4) Competition among us has been shameful.

5) There has been a surfeit of narcissism, battering, demands.

6) I am not your handmaiden.

"It got to the point where the pain in my shoulders has increased each time I talked to one of my Seder Sisters.

"I hope that what will be shared between us tonight will enable all of us to say what is on our minds and then, perhaps, we can come together and heal and devise a strategy that will enable us to go to Jerusalem."

In Lilly's loft, Chesler sits rigidly; Bea and Edith are preoccupied with their own thoughts. They were not informed about the conference or invited to participate.

Lilly is trying something very hard, namely, altering our group character.

I had also prepared a feminist *Miss Manners*. I had thought about the coming meeting and the rancor and came with my own list.

We always seem to be rising and reading manifestos, or making suggestions or listing corrections to our behavior.

> 1) **We must treat each other as peer and equal in our form of address, in our expectations.**
> 2) **We are not children. Therefore, we are not allowed the luxury of childish behavior.**
> 3) **Memory is used to connect and enlarge us, not to add to a list of complaints and betrayals.**

(Who is listening? I'm not sure. Each is studying her own agenda.)

> 4) **Each of us may experience hurt or exclusion, but we refrain from the excesses of retaliation and retribution.**
> 5) **If there is planning that becomes hierarchical and members of the group are not consulted, the planners must know that they may come under siege.**

I end my reading by quoting: "As is written in Mishna, 'When friendships change and continue, they reach a higher plane.'"

Is this wishful thinking? I ask myself. It is the second time we are doing this.

Lilly hands us sweet chocolate to sweeten our way out.

We leave to go our separate ways. Bea and Edith unsmilingly take the elevator up to their loft. The rest of us press the down button. Letty and I put Phyllis into a cab for Brooklyn Heights.

"She attacked me!" Phyllis keeps saying. "She selected me for attack."

She stares stonily before her as the cab heads to the Lower East Side and the bridge to Brooklyn.

Letty drops me off on her way midtown. "Is it the end of us?" I ask.

"The end or a change," says Letty, always practical, never hyperbolic.

It is not the end.

We meet at Lilly's once again. We will discuss the future of
the seder, its structure, and the role each of us wishes to play.
Is it to continue?

First, we each tell how the seders have moved us, altered us.

Then Michele asks, "What upsets us?"

The group members each speak. There has been hurt, too
small a role played by some, too many guests invited by others. We name our pain. Some accuse. Others answer.

No voice is raised.

No one demands or gives an ultimatum.

We decide by consensus to return to intimacy, to have an
egalitarian seder, each one a leader.

We have become grown-ups, about to have our Hai, our
eighteenth birthday.

A New Year's card arrives from Lilly.

> "Dear Esther, It's New Year's Eve. I am finishing
> unfinished business. I just defrosted my fridge and
> cleaned it up. . . . I wanted to say that in our Hai
> year I hope that this seder will be different from all
> other seders, that we can come together like sisters
> in the best sense and create something special,
> mature, building on the shoulders of what you and
> Naomi Nimrod produced . . . bring(ing) to it our
> personal sorrows, values, and politics. . . . As ever,
> Lilly."

 # Remembering

REMEMBERING IS an essential part of Judaism. Indeed, all peoples have their bardic tradition, honoring the warrior and the fallen. We sing of our joy; we keen our grief.

I was remembering my father.

I asked my Seder Sisters to join me in my grief in 1987, as I said the *Kaddish,* the Mourner's Prayer, in an Orthodox synagogue. The women were separated by a curtain from the men's side. My sisters were supportive, even in the difficult circumstances. Several objected strenuously to my "subjecting" myself to this. Nevertheless, they all turned up to be with me as I sang of my dead.

After our early morning service, we gathered in the dining area of the synagogue to plan our next seder.

"Loss" came naturally to my lips.

"Continuity" to Phyllis's, for she had her son Ariel to remind her of the future.

"Loss" was difficult for a theme, and "continuity" was never really addressed.

The seder of 1987 was held at the Canadian Mission. Michele and her daughters sat stunned, still recovering from the death by fire of their grandmother.

"We were all still quite raw from my mother's death," Michele remembered. "We had a photo passed around of her. The topic was too wrenching for me. And Ilana. It was too hard a topic. That made a gloomy occasion. Ariel was uncomfortable. The children couldn't get connected to it."

Grace, who brought her granddaughter Laura, was also unhappy about the seder.

"We felt that the services tended to be too long. And I didn't like the fact that the Seder Sisters didn't seem to like the children. But when the children were asked to say something, they did. Laura put up her hand. She would have talked every time.

"Still," she remembered, "some of the people were very self-indulgent, going on and on. I was very worried about my sisters and that kind of continuity."

Some expressed their loss at that seder, others later to me.

"That was a hard one," said Bella, some time later. "Pretty tough. These are the things you have to go through. It's sometimes like going to a funeral. It's hard to take on more pain when you have your own, but then you say to yourself, 'Some can live with it, release it, and learn from it.' I made a vow I was not going to make any more speeches at people's funerals. My older lawyer friends are dying and I'm not going to speak anymore because it opens my own pain to such a degree that I can't bear it."

Lilly spoke of her mother at the seder: "One week ago my mother had a massive stroke. On Thursday, as I walked to the subway station, I found myself crying on the street. I had been thinking of Bella Rivlin, my mother, thinking of her nearly twenty-four years ago when she came to visit me at Berkeley and we drove to the Seattle World's Fair and had adventures, just the two of us, like girlfriends. For a moment I thought that I couldn't walk on, but I knew very well that I had to go to work, get on with it, and I continued. Loss and Continuity.

"I sat by my mother's bedside. Her face was swollen, I could barely recognize her. Only her cheekbones gave evidence to the beauty that she was. Her lusterless eyes stared up into space. Occasionally she responded. When I bent over her and tried to get her attention, she pushed my hair out of my eyes with her left hand, the only hand she could move. I knew she recognized me and was repeating an old action. 'Lilly, get your hair out of your eyes,' had been her constant refrain as I was growing up. Loss and Continuity."

How does one deal with loss, with death, and make it bearable? We did not succeed.

There was a moment afterward when both Michele and Grace remembered Bella dealing with the children.

"Bella spoke so softly," said Grace. "It was really loving."

"Bella was lovely," said Michele.

We asked if the children had any questions for the adults.

Cory, the daughter of the playwright, Karen Malpede, raised her hand and asked Bella, "Why is there war and how do we stop it?"

Bella leaned forward. Usually her voice rang out strongly and her arms punctuated the air. This time she leaned toward the children: Cory; Ariel Braunshtein; Laura Paley; Anna Cash, daughter of Mary Gordon.

Bella said, "Sometimes on a block there is a big bully. He takes your toys away. He hits you. He makes you cry. How do we handle the bully? How do we make him stop? We isolate him. And then, together, we stop him."

As always, some of the sedergoers were touched; others were not.

Grace was philosophical about the seders: "You have to expect that every couple of seders will be a dead bust. If one doesn't work, don't give in."

# The Covenant

PHYLLIS CHESLER said, in 1988, "Now that we are thirteen, we are not Batei Mitzvah, Daughters of the Mitzvah. We are Mothers of the Deed, and it is incumbent upon mothers to work for peace, to save their sons and daughters from war."

Bella said, "The theme should be, Returning the Soul to the Jewish People, helping them remember their purpose."

Phyllis wanted us to bless one another.

At the seder, I said:

> I am blessed with these women in my life
> and the years we spent together
> and to be blessed by them is an honor.
>
> Mother of the Deed,
> we do this deed solo,
> but better in concert.
> Then, it seems natural and fitting,
> that we should bless one another.

Then Phyllis wants us to ask to be empowered.

Grace objects. She doesn't like the word *power*, the idea of power.

Later she says, "My trouble with the word *power* is that it needs a preposition after it. What do you want power for? To make the world better? When the people receive the power, if they don't know what their preposition is, that isn't good.

"At the beginning of the women's movement I was reading Kropotkin. He came back to Russia after traveling everywhere in the nineteenth century, and he said the only movement worthwhile is the women's movement. The younger women were going around teaching the serfs to be equal persons in the great struggles in the world, changing the life of the oppressed people."

That is using power.

There was a Power Creature in the corner that Lilly and Phyllis had constructed around a clothes rack: the old-fashioned hat of someone's mother on top, photos attached, a piece of jewelry, other totems. There were letters, intimate items of our mothers attached to her. "She" stood in the corner supervising our seder.

Another totemic item was our Sacred Schmata. This, 1988, is the sixth year of our Sacred Schmata.

Phyllis takes her schmata out of its bag.

First she entwines us and reminds us of our history with these scarves.

Then Phyllis says, "It is time to burn the Sacred Schmata, for our power is not in the external but in ourselves."

And she throws it into the fireplace in the Canadian Mission.

At this, Letty bursts into tears.

"No! It is our history!"

And she pulls the schmata from the fire, gathering it to her bosom.

"I had no idea at the moment what happened," she would recount. "I have a lot of trouble with loss because I lost my mother so young. I've lost a lot that meant something to me, her paintings, her things. I have so little of my mother. Things matter to me as symbols, not what something costs. The schmata theatened to be another symbolic loss." She laughs. "But I have it in a drawer and I know it's only an ugly schmata."

Thus it was resolved at the seder that the Sacred Schmata become an Artifact, connecting us, sacred to us and not to be destroyed.

We each have different feelings about that seder.

I had brought in various references, songs, psalms.

Grace said, "I like people bringing in text. There were people of interest at that Thirteenth Seder, like Francine Klagsburn. I like the touch of texts coming in from various people. Church people, Black people, they would love the old language. They are interested in the struggle to become something else."

Michele said, "I loved this second seder at the Mission. There wasn't the theme of death and it was more festive.

Chesler made a wonderful contribution with her funny model/icon."

Gloria said, "That Thirteenth Seder was our worst. We got out of talking as women and got into talking as nationalists. Nationalism invades us.

"Jewish women should continue meeting but with more discussion of the external pressure, the bias, the division among Jews. We should start other groups, supported by having a womanly place in the Jewish tradition.

"As for me," said Gloria, "I think of myself as more refugee than community."

Gloria will change her life.

"My community has been totally work-oriented. Now the children of *Ms.* kids are grown up: the Pogrebin girls, Robin Morgan's son, Suzanne Levine's two little ones. There are a dozen kids and it's become a way to make a family for me."

Gloria is looking for a different center, in her dwelling, in herself.

"Making a family with friends," says Gloria, "being a host instead of always a guest."

But the rest of us continue to try to make order and meaning between "us," focusing on the seder as the paradigm.

The Prevailing Silence

"FINALLY!" SAYS Michele, a deep lover of books, "a literary seder!"

Letty has a prepublication copy of Judith Plaskow's *Standing Again at Sinai* (San Francisco: HarperSanFrancisco, 1990).

That will be our homework, our touchstone.

Over the phone, Letty and I summarize the book: Omission, Absence, Silence.

Each of the Seder Sisters and guests will meditate upon one of those three themes.

We gather at Bea's and, like good schoolgirls, each of us is carrying Plaskow's book.

Adrienne Cooper has agreed to come. Several of the Seder Sisters have heard her perform at the Public Theatre in a Yiddish musical. We have heard her in concert. She is rich-voiced, curly haired, expressive, just what we weak-voiced Sisters need.

Adrienne has met with me to talk about the "program" and the appropriate music for Yiddish songs.

"Yiddish," says Adrienne, "is the only language that doesn't have an army."

Adrienne was a doctoral student at the University of Chicago and active in the Yiddish theater.

"People in Yiddish theater," she said, "are quick to feel anger and affection for each other. Intimacy is part of the culture."

She looks forward to intimacy in the group. She is used to groups. She worked at YIVO, the Yiddish Institute, and is now employed at the Chinese-American Museum in Chinatown.

"*Die zelbe zach,* the same thing," she says. "Only different people and a different language."

♦　♦　♦　♦

I begin: "Miriam has been with us for fourteen years, and she is still in our midst. As Plaskow writes of the prophet Miriam, 'This surprising silence suggests that there were other Miriam traditions that were excluded from the Torah. . . . Tantalizing things are all that's left.'

"Once, says Plaskow, women functioned as 'singers and dancers, diviners and dream interpreters, mourners and priestesses.' "

I continue. "We have been none of these but we will be. It has been a painful path for women of faith, for we are walking against the wind and our words are blown back into our mouth. . . . We women have little effect on the practice of morality, on the language of liturgy, on the hierarchical structure of the house of worship.

"So we have two choices, as the Talmudists would say: One, we can elbow our way into the crowd at the foot of Sinai. . . . Or, we can create new ways . . . and make our own covenantal way."

Lilly says that we have this seder "so we would hear our own voices, so we could name our own experiences, tell our own story, be the main actors in the retelling of the Exodus."

Judith Plaskow and her partner, the historian Martha Acklesberg, are our honored guests, sitting shyly and quietly.

Michele, Edith, and Bea speak on Omission.

Michele has spent the morning in her little West Village apartment writing *Omission:*

> Omit. I brood on this word . . . until the O of *Omit* grows huge, a zero swallowing us up into nothingness.
>
> When our female lives are obliterated from our sacred writing, as though we were nothing, how can we take this empty circle, this hollow place at the core of religion . . . and fill it with meaning?
>
> I look into our long past, and everywhere I search I find the O of omission or obliteration.
>
> Maybe, like Miriam, we will not live to cross into our promised land. But maybe our daughters and sons will eat the sweet grapes of equality there.

Edith Isaac-Rose has filled the loft with her *miraclos,* paintings based on the offerings in Mexican churches, depictions of body parts: legs, arms, mouths. She has painted mouths that face us, open as if to speak, but nothing issues forth.

Edith speaks for the women artists omitted from museums and galleries, not considered grown-ups in the world of art.

Bea talks about the lack of awareness of lesbian women, as if they were not part of the Jewish community, of society at large. That was the cry on the first night when we met in 1976, and that is still the cry, the need, fifteen years later in 1990.

On Silence, I quote from Plaskow's book: "The need for a feminist Judaism begins with hearing silence. . . . Hearing silence is not easy."

It is Letty who speaks of the silent victims of the Hebrew Bible in a beautiful *midrash*:

> I am here to break the silence of Jephthah's Daughter—one of forty daughters in the Hebrew Bible who is identified only by her father's name. I want to bring this young woman into our seder circle tonight. . . .
>
> The story of Jephthah's daughter requires a sorrowful *midrash*. Her story unfolds in Judges 11, and it begins, of course, with the story of a man.

The story is that, to bring victory in battle, Jephthah swears to sacrifice whatever comes out of the door of his house to greet him. That is his daughter.

> We have many questions for God: Why did you allow an innocent girl to be sacrificed in your name?. . .
>
> When Abraham prepared to sacrifice his son Isaac . . . you stayed Abraham's hand and Isaac lived. . . .
>
> God, why did you save the son and let the daughter die?
>
> We cannot accept the narrator's story as the whole story. . . . The real story of Jephthah's daughter lies in us daughters all . . . where the truth about fathers and daughters is made bearable by hope and where we dream of more love from our fathers than most of us have ever known.

Edith names as her models the Gorilla Girls, activist women artists who wear gorilla costumes and do "guerrilla" actions, including political posters that suddenly appear all over Soho, the Village South of Houston, and elsewhere, stating the statistics on representation of women, naming galleries that discriminate against women and minorities. Their posters alone are works of art.

"What kind of outrageous action must one perform to be noticed?" Edith asks.

Her color field paintings are hanging on the wall above our heads, noticed and appreciated.

Bella then comments on our assigned book. She has read, underlined, studied. But she is puzzled.

"Why do we need, yet again, reformation and not transformation?"

She and Judith Plaskow engage in theological dispute about new ways of talking about God when Gloria joins in.

"There are new ways of talking about God/Goddess," says Gloria. "The Goddess was one, whole. She has been broken, torn apart. It is up to us to put her together, to have wholeness, a unity in the universe."

It is time for the group to break the silence, to speak of the silence in their own lives, where they were unheard, ignored, unheeded.

Bella and Manhattan Borough President Ruth Messinger speak of omission; omission of women from the political scene, both politicians having fought long and hard for their careers.

Bella tells us, "It is almost impossible to unseat an incumbent who is usually a male."

Ruth Messinger talks about the disappointment to her family when she, a daughter, was born.

"Next time," a relative comforted the mother, "maybe it will be a boy."

The ceremony is about to conclude.

Robin Pogrebin asks, "How do we bring this special day into the rest of the year, integrate it with our lives?"

Someone opens the apartment door for the Prophet Miriam and Adrienne sings her in.

The Change Makers

THE WHOLE YEAR, 1991, has been drafty, politically and personally, a chill on both the nation and the Seder Sisters.

We had the shock of seeing the "gag rule" pass the Supreme Court and not being overridden by the Senate. No physician, no health worker in a federally funded health clinic can give abortion information to a client. The option of free choice will be hidden in the clinics from the poor and the young.

We had the shock of the administration-sponsored nominee for the Supreme Court testifying, and one could not help but wonder at his veracity when he claimed he had never discussed controversial cases.

Then he was confronted with the careful testimony of Anita Hill. We Seder Sisters watched, along with the nation, while the law professor was insulted by the Senate Judiciary Committee, accused of cribbing her "script" from the horror film, *The Exorcist,* or of writing a book about her adventures. Or was she a lovelorn woman, merely avenging herself? (Michele in Canada said that Canadians also watched fascinated and horror-struck.) Then we heard the vote, wherever we were.

I was teaching in the MFA program at CUNY and one of my students brought his radio and we postponed class to hear the count. The women students burst into tears as the new appointee slithered into the empty chair on the Court.

We had the shock of the federal government coming down on the side of the fundamentalists, who, in St. Louis, were violent against the users of abortion clinics. The Attorney General, Dick Thornburgh, overrode the presiding judge's rule restraining Operation Rescue.

It was as if the courts and the federal government were let loose against us.

The Gulf War had ended, but we Seder Sisters were shocked at the information that came out afterwards, the thousands who were killed and the Iraqi babies dying from malnutrition. And we are still split on the subject.

This year we also had the shock of the depression. Some of us, among the Seder Sisters, were comfortable, at the top of their professions and some were couples with two wage earners. Others of us were artists freelancing or retirees or adjuncts.

And some of our grown-up children could not afford health insurance. Nor could some of the Seder Sisters.

There were more disappointments. Liz Abzug ran for City Council and was defeated in an ugly battle. It also split the women's movement in New York between those who worked for and against her.

"I thought it was about continuity, mother and daughter," said Bella angrily. "I worked for all those women, put their names on our list and they forget. They had amnesia. It was about passing on the torch to the next generation."

The pre-planning meeting is, as usual, at Letty's high ceilinged apartment with flowers everywhere.

"This is the most beautiful place in New York," Michele declares, and she should know for she has explored the city.

It is Letty, high-energy, intelligent, with a glorious smile, who gives us the second theme.

All these years, we have been our own change makers. With Letty's suggestion, we open our seder to those who have marked our lives, the lives of those around them.

Adrienne Cooper comes again. She sings a *nigun,* a wordless Hasidic song, and "Lalala, aiaiai's" us into the circle on the floor.

The circle is enlarged and varied because of the addition of the Change Makers. These are not women handing out change in nickels, dimes, and quarters. This is a classy crowd: writers, newscasters, educators, activists, women of the spirit.

The Orthodox women Change Makers have not attended such a seder, though all their lives they attended seders. Marilyn French and her daughter, Jamie French, and Carol Jenkins, New York NBC-TV anchorperson and her daughter, Elizabeth II, have also not attended such a seder or any seder. Nor, strangely enough, has Carolyn Heilbrun, née Gold, who, though Jewish, never participated in a Jewish holiday.

The room is filled with the young, some of whom were chosen to be honored, for, as Bella said, "There has to be a passing on of the torch."

And the room is filled with the dignified mature who have lit the torch.

I describe the holiday for those who have not known such a holy day: "There is a pentimenti in this holiday of two pagan holidays of thousands of years ago."

At this Gloria Steinem looks interested. She has felt in recent years as some of us became more faithful that we were too God-ridden and not thinking enough about the millennia of the Goddess. The Orthodox women, at the other end of the room, seem to be blinking.

"The holidays were the shepherding-lambing season and the barley harvest. There were even limping dances in the earliest days, simulating the weak-legged lamb rising. There was unleavened cake eaten, made of barley, long before wheat was sown."

I speak of Miriam:

"Miriam is caretaker rather than searcher; predicter rather than actor. She is the angry one who cries out for her own justice. She argues with God, who scorns her as an errant child. . . . This is God's eleventh plague, the giving of the only prophet from the House of Levy leprosy and then, seven days later, curing her.

"She dies in *Kadesh,* which means 'holy,' but what does it mean to be holy if one is a woman?"

I then welcome historical characters as well as our present guests:

> Welcome Eve, the Mother of All Living.
> Welcome the Princess of Israel, Sarah, and the
> Egyptian Hagar, who shared the tent.
> Welcome to She Who Turned to Look Back.
> Welcome to the First Prophet of All, Miriam,
> Bitterness of her People.
> Welcome to those Egyptian and Hebrew women

who saved the wailing baby in the papyrus basket
and called him, He Who Is Pulled Out.
Welcome to the sister, the mother, the foster mother.
You, our forebears, have taught us well to care for
one another.
Welcome, seven daughters of the Priest of Midian.
Welcome, Bird Woman, Zipporah, the wife of
Moses, the woman who tricked God, the Divine
Demon.
Welcome to all our congregants who gather in a
circle to tell the untold tale.

We lean to the left, for, as Chesler says, "We are still in
slavery. Women lean on each other for support. And we still
have twenty-three years left in the desert, for we are only in
our seventeenth year of searching our way. And it takes the
proverbial forty."

Michele welcomes the Change Makers with *Perkei Ima'ot,*
or the Words of the Mothers in Praise of Their Prophets:

"We welcome our sisters, the Change Makers, and
we call them prophets, and, in the words of Isaiah,
indignation rained down into your souls, and you
became prophets—those who speak truth in public.

"You scorned to stay indoors, embroidering your
well-being, crooning, 'Peace, peace in the house,'
where there is no peace outdoors. . . .

"You abominated injustice, hated silly lies, went
forth to teach the young with clarity and passion
. . . walked on stony paths, reached out the hand of
sisterhood to those without speech, and braved the
scorching fire of the enemy's words. . . .

"The women honor you, and all our million
nameless prophets before you. . . ."

I introduce Carol Jenkins as the first Change Maker. She
has been on local NBC-TV for twenty years, since very
young. Her intelligence comes across large but also intimate-
ly on our screens.

I have walked with her and seen passengers leap from their
car to thank her. In Harlem pushcart tenders whispered,

"You grace the race."

Carol speaks briefly about coming to this seder with her daughter and taking seats that are, coincidentally, on the outer edge of the circle: "Bella saw my daughter and me sitting here and she said, 'Are you sitting in the back of the bus? Well, then, I guess I have to join you,' and she took the next seat."

I had wanted Carol to say how her work had taken her to places and how she had taken her work to further destinations. When sent to Mother Hale, who kept a boarding house for crack babies, Carol adopted a child.

Working on another story, sent to a crowded tenement, Carol met an articulate, lively boy. "Take him!" said his mother, pushing him at Carol. "Save him." Carol took him in and tried to help him.

Carol's daughter, Elizabeth, a student at Hotchkiss preparatory school, wrote an editorial for the school newspaper against racism and anti-Semitism after hearing anti-Semitic remarks by a fellow student.

"We are a small school," Elizabeth said at the seder, "and what hurts one, hurts us all."

She will be part of the Third Wave, young feminists, going by bus to twenty cities, registering voters across the land.

Letty Cottin Pogrebin glowingly describes Janet Barrett, who gave her the concept for this theme.

"When I went into her classroom in the Bronx, the students arrived bent over. As soon as she began talking they straightened up, shook themselves out of their despair. She gave them dignity, pride."

Janet Barrett says, "I grew up in the projects. I had a poor self-image. I always thought, wherever I was, that I couldn't do any better, and then I went on up to the next place and did better, until I went to college and I wondered why I was there until I graduated. And then I took graduate work. And then I knew why I was there and came back to teach others."

Gloria Steinem introduces her Change Makers, the novelist and scholar Marilyn French and the scholar-professor-mystery writer Carolyn Heilbrun.

Marilyn French was Mara Solwoska. Carolyn Heilbrun, née Gold, is also Amanda Cross, author of mysteries about a distinguished English professor who solves crimes by explicating text.

We contemplate all the name changes women go through, some being named once, twice, some choosing their own.

Marilyn's book *The War Against Women* (New York: Summit Books, 1992), is due out. From her vast research and knowledge, Marilyn gives a mini–history lesson on the small handful of Hebrew families hiding in the mountains from the militaristic, tax-collecting state that Egypt had become. And that handful became a tribe and left the oppressive land.

"I've always felt an affinity for them," says Marilyn.

Carolyn Heilbrun has serious news for the gathered. Perhaps being in a circle of women gives her strength to announce it.

"It has become unbearable for me at Columbia University," she tells us.

Some of us are startled. Her reputation is so great. She is one of the treasures of Columbia.

"A woman deserving of appointment was turned down and, in her stead, a mediocre man was selected," says Carolyn. "I find, more and more, that I have to teach my students to use euphemisms to disguise the feminism in their work. The president of Columbia always refers to me when he says, 'See! We have a feminist English department.' I can no longer bear being a token." Carolyn Heilbrun looks around the room.

"I have tendered my resignation."

We gasp. We toast her with one of the four requisite cups of wine, for courage.

Edith Isaac-Rose introduces Phyllis Kriegel, publisher of *New Directions for Women*. Both Kriegel and Merle Hoffman, publisher of *On the Issues,* are honored tonight for their valuable work in having alternative presses that provide information about women that is not readily accessible.

Kriegel tells of the life of her generation in the suburbs, in Westchester, making dinners. The social life of dinner parties was the be-all and end-all.

Says Kriegel, "No wonder Judy Chicago named her sculpture piece *The Dinner Party.*"

Women have come out of the kitchen, away from the table, to the world of work and good works.

Bea Kreloff introduces Edith Konecky.

"We were women of long marriages," says Bea, "mine twenty-four, Edith Konecky's twenty, but we were different, lesbians, Jewish, family people all that dark time ago. Konecky wrote two novels, thinly disguised autobiographies about the experience we both shared, mothers, lesbians of an older generation. The separation, isolation, longing of that time is described in her books."

Chesler has brought the women who were active in Solidarity with Jewish Women at the Western Wall as her Change Makers.

These women, Chesler, I, and others at the Empowerment of Jewish Women Conference in 1988 held an action. We were the first women to take the Torah to the Wall. Our reception was violent on the part of the *haredi*, the ultra-Orthodox, but the excitement this action engendered in other women, in Israelis, made them continue to claim their sacred space. The police do not protect them, but they continue going in a group. Their suit to have a right to worship together is before the Israeli Supreme Court, which is dragging its feet.

Chesler has been active all this time with these women. Connecting yourself to a wall firms you up.

There was an intrafaith support service in New York in 1989, where, in a rare united front, all the branches of Judaism were represented.

Against the voices of the leading rabbis in Israel, the women issued their own statement.

The rabbis had called the women who prayed, "Liliths" and said that "when women pray together, the Shekhinah is not present," and, "This is the work of satan and women's liberation."

The women wrote:

> To express our solidarity with women wishing to pray at the *Kotel* (Western Wall) . . . in Jerusalem; wishing to pray in accordance with Jewish law, in peace and in safety. We are . . . Orthodox, we are Conservative, we are Reconstructionist, we are Reform, we are secular, we are unaffiliated. We share . . . a strong concern about our sisters in

Israel, who suffer humiliation, violent attack, and abuse when they go to the *Kotel* to pray.

Rivke Haut, Founder of Women's *Tefillah* (Prayer) Network in Brooklyn, looks around our loft at the gathered sedergoers.

"This is the first time Orthodox women have joined with you. The violence of men has brought us together."

"Torah (the Five Books of Moses) brought us together," says Susan Aranoff.

Dr. Susan Aranoff is head of *Agunah*. This organization deals with the matter of Orthodox Jewish women unable to receive a divorce from their husbands and held in legal limits. Dr. Aranoff distributes a Passover plea:

> As you sit down to your festive seder, a celebration of our freedom, we call upon you to remember *agunot,* women who are denied their freedom by husbands who hold them captive by refusing to grant them religious divorces. . . . As we remember the affliction of our people enslaved in Egypt, we join with *agunot* and experience a taste of the bitterness of their lives.

We, sitting in a circle, all dip *karpas,* parsley, in saltwater to think of their tears.

Phyllis introduces Merle Hoffman, who, besides editing a publication, also runs a birth and abortion center, Choices.

Merle says, "I have held the hands of women having abortions before. I will hold their hands again, but it will soon be illegal to have an abortion in this country."

Although she is one of us, we honor our own Bella.

"Bella," I say, "is our chief Change Maker. We honor her for the change she wrought in all of our lives."

Bella says, "In the Zionist youth movement I belonged to, *Hashomer HaTzair,* we used to sing *Hazak v'Amatz,* strength and courage."

We sing this song and toast her with another of our four cups.

There are two young Change Makers, about thirty years old.

Rivlin has declared Naomi Wolf her Change Maker.

Naomi authored *The Beauty Myth* (New York: William Morrow, 1991), making young women aware of the social pressures, turning the next generation toward feminism.

Naomi, in turn, honors Lilly as her mentor.

In a few weeks Naomi will deliver a commencement address at Scripps College, warning and advising the young women graduates. We Seder Sisters are not the only advisers in the land.

Naomi Wolf gives her advice to the graduates:

> Ask for money. . . . Whatever field your heart decides on . . . get the most specialized training.
>
> Never cook for or sleep with anyone who routinely puts you down. . . .
>
> Become goddesses of disobedience. . . . (*New York Times,* Op Ed, May 31, 1992).

Claudia Weinstein is introduced by Nahama. She has been to previous seders, but now she is honored as a professional with a conscience. Reporting for The *American Lawyer,* Claudia investigated the condition of illegal aliens, held in the desert in the Southwest, without access to legal aid. Laws were changed as a result, and Claudia was honored for her reporting. She is now associate producer for "Sixty Minutes."

Adrienne Cooper sings Miriam in the door:

> Miriam *ha nevia* (the prophet)
> Miriam *m'bet ha Levy* (from the House of Levy)
> soon will come to us (x3)
> with timbrel and song.

## PART FIVE

Community

The Ceremonies of Community

FOR MORE THAN fifteen years we have been present for one another for birthing ceremonies, re-empowerment ceremonies, to comfort after heartbreak, to reassure after a hysterectomy, to be there when hearing of the loss of a parent.

As with Bella's Hug-In, the seder women knew how to honor and nurture one another, and we did it dramatically.

1978. FOR PHYLLIS. AFTER THE CIRCUMCISION.
On January 13, 1978, I flew from Detroit to New York for a ceremony: "Returning the Boy Child to the Women of the Family."

Phyllis had asked me to perform the ceremony after the circumcision of her new son, Ariel. She knew that, during the circumcision, the name of the father and all the illustrious male ancestors back to the tenth generation would be spoken. But none of the women who had borne the illustrious sons of the family would be mentioned by name. They were mere conduits.

Phyllis had phoned me at Wayne State University to request that I retrieve the child from the men and return him to the women of the family.

Chesler's apartment on West End Avenue was celebratory, with a table laid with delicatessen fare, with bagels, cheeses, honey cakes, and schnapps whiskey, for a *l'haim,* a toast to life.

Besides the father, the *mohel,* the one to circumcise, and the father's friends, stood the contigent of women: Phyllis, her mother, her aunt, her friends, including Erica Jong, who drove in from Connecticut, in the early stages of her pregnancy, and Gloria Steinem, who flew in from Washington, D.C., where she was on a writing grant. New York women, like publicist Selma Shapiro, lent their presence to this ritual.

After the baby was circumcised and the tiny yarmulke was

placed on his head and he was told, "Now you're a Jew," I said, "It is time for us."

We took the baby away from the men.

We crowded into the study, sitting in a tight circle.

I introduced Ariel's grandmother and aunt to the group.

"The rest of us are his godmothers," I said.

Around the room the women blessed him.

"May you be tender," I said, "and, although you bruise, may you not bruise others."

Others said, "May you never feel more pain than you do on this day of circumcision."

"May you be strong enough to be the son of a feminist."

"May your mother be your friend all your shared life." It was Gloria, I believe, who blessed him that way.

"I bless you with laughter. You will need it."

"May you honor the women of your life as we honor you."

I asked that we present Ariel with something both useful and magical, a growing part of ourselves, whether it be a strand, curl, tendril, a nail clipping. For we were gathered here to weave together, to thatch, to patch.

I pulled out my tape, scissors, and card of red oaktag paper.

"This will be for Ariel in case he ever needs a spell, god-spell, magic," I said.

I cut the first strand of hair from my head and taped it upon this page of life and passed down the card. Each woman present cut her hair for Ariel—the gray of his grandmothers and aunt, black of his mother, blond of Gloria, brown of Erica.

We lit candles for Ariel and presented him with this hairy card of great power.

1979. FOR BELLA. AFTER THE FIRING.
It was the next year, 1979.

I would meet Bella Abzug as a result of Firing Friday, when, in Washington, on January 12th, President Jimmy Carter fired Bella. She had been co-chair of his National Advisory Committee on Women.

She had raised the funding for a meeting in Houston, Texas, the National Women's Conference, which would spawn a generation of new women politicians.

Hamilton Jordan, before Bella's meeting with Carter,

phoned the press, "Boys, wanna have some fun? We're gonna fire Bella!"

The press was already gathered when Bella, unknowing, spoke to President Carter about the effect on women when there were cuts in social programs while the defense budget was being increased.

Her tone was strident, her finger employed like that of a *melamed,* a teacher. Neither the New York voice nor the pointing index finger pleased the southern president. It was not how ladies comported themselves.

Her firing in 1979 by the president had some of the effect of the treatment of Anita Hill by the Senate Judiciary Committee in 1991, shock at the arrogance of office holders.

In Detroit there was a luncheon to honor her work on women's behalf and to hear her story. I was to be poet laureate and sat at her table.

She said to us at her table, "Know what that ___ Jordan told me? He said, 'You know why (your husband) Martin is ill? You never stayed home. He had one heart attack already. You should stay home and take care of him.'"

That was January 30th, 1978, when I rose and read Bella a New Ten Commandments.

"These are the Male Commandments," I said:

1) **Thou shalt not replace a man in Congress.**
2) **Thou shalt not run for Senate.**
3) **Thou shalt not have opinions before the president.**
4) **Thou shalt not be of energy and ambition.**
5) **Thou shalt not have a history of successful endeavor.**
6) **Thou shalt not spread compassion from outside thine own house, especially not unto the poor, the tired, the weary, the Black, the women, the gays.**
7) **Thou shalt have no vision, and if thou hast, let it be tunnel vision.**
8) **Thou shalt not raise thy voice above men, for in doing so, we would distract them from prayer and power.**
9) **Thou shalt not enter a room surrounded by friends, but singly, modestly, inconspicuously.**
10) **Thou shalt not let defeat strengthen thee.**

I said to the women of Detroit, "We must be Tablet Breakers and New Rule Makers. Thou Shalt Not was written by men. This is how women speak:

1) **Thou shalt enter the ancient Forbidden City of Washington, D.C.**
2) **Thou shalt replace the marble statues and oil portraits of men with the living presence of women.**
3) **Thou shalt honor thy women leaders that their days be long in the land.**
4) **Thou shalt educate thy daughters and honor them as we do our sons.**
5) **Thou shalt write and recite thine own history and place our founding mothers within its covers.**
6) **Thou shalt work mightily at replacing those who dishonor thee, whether they be from the city, the state, or head of the party.**
7) **Thou shalt remove those from office who would remove thee from the right to thine own body.**
8) **Thou shalt become as an army in the land.**
9) **Thou shalt invoke the names of thy foremothers: the judge Deborah, the warriors Yael, Judith, and the mighty Bella.**
10) **Thou shalt go forth with timbrel and song to right the ancient wrong.**

Yet, it would be Bella who was to work at connecting the Carter-Kennedy forces at the next Democratic convention, so all could unite behind President Carter.

But some of us could not forget the need to humiliate the bravest and best of us.

1982. FOR A SEDER SISTER. AFTER HEARTBREAK. SITTING SHIVAH FOR A LOST LOVE.

One Seder Sister has a broken heart.

Her lover, sixty-three, has gone to find a woman, twenty-three. Our friend, forty-three, thinks life is over, unfair; it's a man's world.

She cannot cease from weeping.

Her features are dissolving in the saltwater.

Her coloring has changed to boiled red.

She, a great beauty, has dulled her eyes, her hair, her soul.

So we gather to sit *shivah,* to hold a wake, on the day the lover weds his young woman.

We bring two items with us: a tape recorder and a cooked chicken.

We sit in a circle and speak into the machine.

We remind the bereaved of truth.

We remind the bereaved of her lost self.

We correct memory.

We reclaim the past.

The friend has been swept away. We must regather her, sweep her up, bring her back to us.

We remind our friend of who she is, how she is still whole.

We each remember the lost love. We correct our friend's memory.

We embrace in holy circle. We drink wine to the reunited wholeness of our friend.

We acknowledge amputation, separation as part of life.

We eat the cooked chicken. Ordinary routines go on.

We speak of work, of dreams, of visions.

The friend weeps and is embraced, and the tears wash away loss.

Our friend may wear a sign of mourning, besides her reddened eyes and heaving chest.

We cut a black armband and give it to our friend with a finite time in which to mourn.

And to end it.

1984. FOR ESTHER. AFTER THE OPERATION.
In Spring of 1984 I had a hysterectomy. My children came to bid farewell to their former abode, the twin sons complaining that it had been crowded in there.

I was dressed in white like a bride.

A *minyan,* a group of ten, women in this case, led by Phyllis and Lilly, gathered at our loft, carrying fruit—figs and dates, apricots and nuts, the firstfruits of the season for it was *Shavuoth,* the Holiday of Weeks, the time of first harvest.

The women placed me in the center of their circle and fed me as they said I had fed others, inside me and around my table.

Then the *minyan* of women spoke on:

Having a Womb and Using It
Having a Womb and Losing It
Having a Womb and Not Using It

And we spoke of what happens to one's womb—the fruit of the womb, firstfruit aborted, uterine cancer.

And we also spoke of what we suffered to be feminine— the boned, wired bras; the large curlers that strained our necks as we tried to straighten our hair.

And we declared an end to bone, wire, and plastic as a way of enhancing our beauty.

Then the women declared me Crone and said that the words I would utter would henceforth be considered wise.

A womb is like an accordian, expanding for as many as are contained within it. We declared an external womb, with which to care for, to aid those in need.

1987. FOR ESTHER. IN MOURNING.

My father died in 1987. He was a journalist, a gentle man. My father expected the *Kaddish,* the Mourner's Prayer, to be said for him by his sons, for daughters are not customarily the *Kaddish* of their parents.

I, the eldest, did not wish to abdicate my responsibility. The only place one could mourn daily was in an Orthodox synagogue.

I phoned one in the neighborhood.

"Oh," said the voice on the telephone, "we don't allow our women to mourn."

I thought of women with brimming eyes and fixed smiles.

I found a place nearby to say my Kaddish prayer.

But the men did not welcome my daily presence and hid themselves from me by turning their backs on me or hid me from them by pulling a curtain across the women's bench in our tiny prayer room.

I had been there for some weeks, either embattled or slowly making a few allies, when I decided to have an action.

I wrote my Seder Sisters and others at the beginning of March.

> Dear Minyan Mates:
> As most of you know, I have been saying *Kaddish* for my father for six weeks at an Orthodox *shul*. It's been an education for all of us. I, who am counted or discounted as half-a-man, the others who thought they were safe on an island of males.
> I now need you, my sisters. I wish to have a *minyan* of women to attend the mourning service, Sunday, March 29th (1987).

Michele said, "I vowed I would never go to a synagogue that separated the men from the women, but, for Esther, I went. I know what it is to lose a parent and to need to mourn."

My sisters came: Letty with her hair primly back; Michele rushing down from the Upper East Side; Bea, from Westbeth, annoyed that I, a feminist, had placed myself in such a position. Edith walked over from her studio on 14th. Phyllis hired a car and drove in from Brooklyn early in the morning. Lilly Rivlin took time out from her busy schedule and new job at New Israel Fund to come to *shul*. Nahama came to add her voice to my *Kaddish*.

Bella was not going to be in town. "I said *Kaddish* for my father when I was thirteen all those years ago," she said, "when I was a girl and nobody did it. And I found out I would do what I needed to do and nobody could stop me. Next time you need me, call upon me and I'll come."

We filled the room with our presence and our voices.

When the prayers were finished, I sponsored a *kiddish,* with lox and herring and bagels and the men rushed into the room to eat. Some took little packets of food home with them to their lonely apartments.

"Remember how it was," one fellow said to the others, "when the women would come afterwards and make a spread and it was so comfortable?"

I was to stay the course, another nine months, strength-ened by that memory of the women claiming their ancient right to mourn.

1988. FOR PHYLLIS. IN SUPPORT.

Lilly called the Seder Sisters, "Phyllis needs support."

Lilly arranges the support session at the Canadian Mission. We are there to join her in a meal. Then we rise, go into the living room, and surround Phyllis. She falls into us, against us. And we protect her. We catch her. Lilly reads instructions about Trust, about Falling, about Getting Up, about Pulling Oneself Up.

Phyllis smiles her radiant smile.

If only we could have permanent effect.

1990. 1991. FOR NAHAMA. THE JOURNEY.

In late July of 1990, Bob and I open the door of our loft to greet wise women and some gentle men. We form a circle around a very pregnant young woman, Nahama, who sits enthroned on a sculptured chair, hand-carved by her brother Adam. She sits there to receive the blessings of the gathered for the ceremony "Blessing the Journey from Water to Air."

Rabbi Pamela Hoffman, a recent graduate of Jewish Theological Seminary, has come to help us expedite. Rabbi Pam reads the angels' blessings, those that surround us: on the right, Michael, God's gift; on the left, Gabriel, the strength of God; behind us, Uriel, the light of God; before us, Raphael, the health of God.

We sing a song by Cantor Debbie Friedman replete with blessings from the *Shekhinah*.

> May you be blessed
> beneath the wings of the *Shekhinah*.
> Be blessed with love,
> be blessed with peace.

And we sing another song from Debbie Friedman (from the tape *You Shall Be a Blessing*, Sounds Write Productions, 1989, available from Jewish Family Productions). The song, with words by Savina Teubal, is based on the words God spoke to Abraham: "Go forth," *Lech Lecha*. It gives women permission to cross borders into the feminine, *Lechi Lach*.

> *L'chi Lach* (f)
> to a land that I will show you
> *Lech L'cha* (m)
> to a place you do not know

L'chi Lach
on your journey I will bless you
and you shall be a blessing
L'chi Lach.

Phyllis Chesler blesses Nahama, stroking her hand and arm, reading from her own memoir, *With Child* (New York: Crowell, 1979), I see a carapace forming around Nahama. I begin to see her taking her place as the person she will be.

All of our friends who are able come to bless her.

Michele writes from Toronto, "I do not believe in God, so I can't be a godmother. But I believe in books, so I'll be her book fairy."

Lilly Rivlin gives her a silver *Chamsa,* a hand amulet, that Lilly has worn as protection. From now on, it will protect Nahama on her journey.

Mary Gordon gives her a Mexican wooden angel to bless her.

And, properly blessed, holding the silver *Chamsa* in her hand, Nahama goes into her hard travail and bears a golden-haired girl.

And there is trouble. Congenital problems.

We phone Letty, who calls a pediatric neurosurgeon in Los Angeles for advice.

Bea and Edith make the soothing sounds of comfort every day on the phone.

Lilly comes one hard night with Chinese take-out for everyone.

About nine months after the initial Journey ceremony, I speak to Cantor Debbie Friedman on the phone to California.

Debbie and I share the keynote speech at the Timbrels of Miriam Conference at the University of Judaism in Los Angeles. By phone and fax, we plan our interweaving of story and song. "The Journey from Water to Air" will be part of the presentation.

"Write another blessing song, using all the angels, to bless my daughter and her daughter," I request.

Debbie writes:

May our right hand draw us closer to our
Godliness.

May our left hand give us strength to face each day.
And before us, may our vision light our paths
ahead.
And behind us, may well-being heal our way.

All around us is Shekhinah.
All around is Shekhinah.

On my right, Michael.
On my left, Gabriel.
And before me, Uriel.
And behind me, Raphael.

All around us is Shekhinah.
All around us is Shekhinah.

There is reprieve. The child grows extraordinarily and, more importantly, normally.

When we have our seder The Plagues We Live Under, Nahama said to the group, "You may think I would list the problems of Alexandra as a plague. But it turned out to be a blessing of friendship. I quote what Letty told me when I asked her for help, 'That's what we're all here for.'"

It takes a lot of communal blessings to make a journey successful, to make one wish come true.

Those are our dramatic appearances for one another.

The Duties of Community

WHEN WE ACT in concert, communally, in accord, we are in the ideal community. This is Utopia. In such a State, we each intuit the others' needs, help them to save face in potentially embarrassing situations, are there totally to rejoice in fortune and to be helpful in misfortune.

It is more fun to rejoice in fortune than misfortune.

At the same time, there is such good grace, good sportswomanship as our health may be shakier, as arthritis or bursitis or neurological problems act up.

The financially insecure keep thinking of wily plans to bridge the gap until the next paycheck.

There are the ordinary requirements of friendship. We honor each other in the concerned phone call, in our applause at a seder sister's performance, or, as Bea always does, in bringing chicken soup.

We are as bad-tempered as the next group of people. Sometimes our voices are shrill or we hang up on the seder sister who has phoned. Sometimes we plot, feel attacked, not recognized by the group. Competition is our nemesis. And it always has to be encountered and negotiated.

Several of us are writers, and the letters and faxes of explanation and continued discussion fly back and forth from Brooklyn to midtown Manhattan, from Toronto to the rest of us in the States. We are never done with clarification.

But, when we are on our best behavior, we are very, very good. There are daily reminders of our duties.

For instance, the Birthday Woman, if she has informed us of that date, receives cards, congratulatory phone calls, a dinner.

And then we simply meet, one to one, when it seems we have lost touch.

There is a group in Berkeley, the writers Nan Fink and her partner, Susan Griffin, tell me, called the Soul Patrol, where a community of friends keep check on one another. That is ideally what we need everywhere. In the meantime, we do the civilized and concerned things we can.

There are Running Meetings, where Lilly and I run along Seventh Avenue from opposite directions, to meet halfway for breakfast and a catch-up of news and to clutch each other's hands for strength.

We are there when Letty is honored by the women's organization Naamat. We cheer when she delivers a brilliant keynote at a *Tikkun* conference in New York or when she and her daughters, Robin and Abigail, present moving speeches on the mother-daughter relationship at another conference. We are there in force for the book party for *Deborah, Golda, and Me,* in which we appear briefly as characters.

We are there for Ariel Chesler Braunshtein's Bar Mitzvah in Brooklyn. After all, some of us had been there at the very beginning.

There are professional acts of friendship, such as Michele's generosity to each of us in helping to promote our books, our films.

There are personal acts of friendship, as Michele hosts us at the Mission or in Toronto, aiding us in our pursuits, contributing to our causes.

There is Gloria flying to Toronto and adding a fund-raiser for the film to her schedule.

Or Bella's playing with baby Alexandra and teaching her to take a punch at life.

"Do this!" commands Bella, punching into the air, "and say, 'Yeah!' And do this!" Punch. "This." Punch. "Yeah, yeah to life."

The baby happily punches her way around the room, "Yeah! Yeah!"

She may need this stance in the world.

We are usually respectful of one another. If Letty phones that she wants to organize a Black-Jewish New York Women's Dialogue, Edith offers her studio for the meeting-place and we all show up. Our dialogue group, with Lilly, Bea, me, and others, lasts for over three years.

When Lilly's films were shown at the Jewish Museum, we were there in the audience. In *Miriam's Daughters Now* we could see ourselves still young as the years moved away from 1984.

◆   ◆   ◆   ◆

We drink tea or dine together. We follow the other's diet—no salty, fatty foods for Bea; no seafood or pork for me.

Bea would come over after teaching, tired and hungry. She is a better cook than I, with an appetite for all of life, but I won't tempt her. I set out nonfattening food, salt-free cheese to keep her blood pressure from climbing. I slice celery and carrots into strips. I go to the farmer's market at Union Square to buy her favorite, crunchy apples.

We start with coffee. Then Bea can lean back. She has been on her feet teaching art.

"Well," says Bea, "they didn't get us."

"They" means those who *reise shticklach,* pull pieces from us, as they say in Yiddish. "They" are the workplace, friends, family, social demands. "They" is also the political scene.

"We've done it again," says Bea. "We got through the week."

Bea's mother died at fifty, so Bea feels that every day from fifty on is a gift. When Bea had a sixtieth birthday, I suggested she rent a barge on the East River. I knew that barge would be bulging, for Bea has a gift for friendship. People would be swimming in its wake, hanging on to the raft. Fish would rise up to gargle, "Happy Birthday."

"How's your health?" I ask.

Bea hurts here and there, the back, sciatica, a leg muscle, an infection in the gums.

"And yours?"

I hurt here, the back, and there, the neck and right shoulder. We exchange the names of physicians, dentists, chiropractors, physical therapists.

We speak of courageous women we know. We speak of necessary political action. Bea might tell me about WAC, Women's Action Coalition, meeting every Tuesday night in Manhattan. I arrive. Twelve hundred women show up, but Bea has saved a chair for me.

We speak of triumphs: successes at work, of her lover's exhibiting work, of my husband Bob about to have a museum show, of my publishing a story, of the sweetness of our families. We speak of hurtful things, great losses: a child not heard from for years, a child depressed, friends who are mortally ill of cancer in the epidemic that is taking beloved women from us.

Bea laughs ruefully about a close friend who suggests that WAC sponsor a "Breastival," a parade of women with bared chests, especially those, including the close friend, who have had mastectomies.

"That's one way to bring attention to the statistics," says Bea.

Dinner with Bea or my Seder Sisters means that within the core of one's heart, the other dwells. We travel to dangerous places with the help of the other. And we safely return to the shore where the other greets us.

We use our resources for the other. We have an Old Girls' Network.

Chesler nominates one of us to go to a United Nations meeting in Oslo with her in 1980. I bring another one of us to the Sinai in 1984 for the Sinai Gathering, an international meeting of people of faith. Lilly is on the planning board for a conference in Jerusalem in 1988 and places two of us on the rostrum.

If we're called upon, we have been known to suggest one or the other of us for a fellowship or professorship.

We make space for one another.

If it is crowded in my apartment with family, Gloria offers a room in her apartment to work in. Letty offers a key to hers.

We have a key to the other in some way.

◆　◆　◆　◆

Because we are so grand in our gestures so often, it is even more hurtful when we are petty, which we are—covetous of the other's success, impatient, judgmental.

We can even make mischief.

When one of us published a book, another said, "But you didn't mention us in it."

When one of us tried to fly, another pulled her down by the ankles.

If one is not given sufficient *koved,* honor, she will be accusatory and enraged.

Another will delay and make the Seder Sisters court her until she participates in the seder.

Some of us are ideologues; some of us are bored by ideologies and actions.

We have all the small faults of petty people and some of the large ones, fissure-sized, seismographic.

But we take the time and have the turn of mind to solve the problems a community faces.

Phyllis Chesler once found a way of negotiation and taught the Seder Sisters.

Her book *Women and Madness* had been ignored for months by the *New York Times* until the poet Adrienne Rich reviewed it for the front page of the *Times Book Review.*

Chesler had so much respect for Rich that when Chesler was embroiled in a dispute over the coauthorship of another book, she persuaded Rich to serve on an unofficial *Beth Din,* the Jewish Court of Law, to pass down judgment on the two quarreling authors. The matter was resolved.

We seder people often had to resolve difficulties ourselves in such a creative, alternative fashion.

Perhaps who we were and how we created ourselves made our development as a group the occasional failure and more frequent triumph it turned out to be.

 # Building Community

EACH OF US was a presence. Chesler was a queenly presence. I seldom saw her leave her apartment and, later, her brownstone without a train of aides, a flock of followers.

Michele was also a presence in Canada. She and Stephen Lewis were the Royal Canadian Couple, Stephen, the heir apparent to the leadership of the New Democratic Party founded by his father. There is no anonymity for them in Canada. Both are recognized on the street and stopped by grateful citizens.

Letty and Gloria had the years with *Ms.* to make them the visible feminists.

But Letty thought of herself as an outsider among the Seder Sisters initially.

"I never thought of it as community because I never had friendships with anyone, just acquaintances," Letty remembered.

Her working and political friendships were with Gloria and Bella. She knew Phyllis well from the early days of the feminist movement. But she described our group as "a single-issue" connection.

"I never felt part of it, I brought food and made phone calls. I never decided themes—only in the last few years. The seder was like the place in the musical *Brigadoon,* appearing once a year and then disappearing."

But, in the last years, Letty made the decision to become more involved in all of us and in the seder.

The pre-planning sessions are dinner events at her home. We are invited for the gatherings around distinguished guests who come to the city, especially in the Israeli peace or feminist movement.

Besides her increasingly active political role, Letty has delved into Jewish studies. She brings all of herself to the group.

Letty thinks about the history of the seder.

"It mirrored the women's movement," she said, "a progenitor/mother torn between pride of authorship and martyrdom. It is a paradigm for an exclusively female structure, not enough slots in the seder.

"What happens at the seder is always magical and satisfying," said Letty, "but on the way, it's often rocky. It all comes out before the seder. There is confusion between the social and the political."

Letty has clarity. There are problems but she loves the seder.

"There is a special intimacy. What I get out of it is an organic Judaism, with an additional feminist incarnation."

The tall stems of flowers reach out of the vases in her living room. The leather couches are soft and pliable.

She smiles, "There is a certain kind of transcendence to it."

◆　◆　◆　◆

Gloria thinks about the seders. "I discovered for the first time the purpose of ritual—to make an open space for emotions to happen. I thought it was wonderful.

"Since I haven't been brought up in this way, I do not think about holiday and I never know when they come.

"Now, I think if we could do ceremony in the beginning of activist meetings, we would be more whole.

"I had never been part of any Jewish or religious ceremony," she said. "In junior high school I went through my own self-created religious experience—Protestant-Congregationalist."

As the seders passed Gloria said, "The magic of the first time didn't strike again for a long time. The meetings were so big. There wasn't enough time for people to speak. It became less of a revelation. I allowed other things to take priority."

Gloria began to absent herself.

"We got out of talking as women and into nationalism. Nationalism invades us. Is there any way we could declare ourselves the Israel for Women and forget about Israel?

"Women is an immigrant group. We have to apply what we have learned about immigrant groups to women, the psychology of the immigrant group."

Each of us came to the group with different needs. Gloria came for community that wasn't only work-oriented. She, feeling refugee, needed sanctuary. We could not always be that.

There were others, Bea for instance, who, like Gloria, opposed nationalism, were internationalists in their orientation. They were also leery of the seders becoming too "God-ridden," as Gloria put it.

But Gloria wanted a language for metaphor, for pilgrimage, an extension outward and inward that was beyond the rationalist approach of others in our group.

We wanted different things: Letty, a deepening Jewish identification; Bea, political activism; I, a belief in the grammar of spirituality, a didactic, pedagogical approach and yet also wanting to taste the honey of lyrics on my tongue and feel the thrill of risking change.

Lilly wanted community—we, family, her native Israel all merged. Phyllis wanted recognition for the large spirit and mind that she is. She wanted family, a family of friends. When there was an emergency with her, she felt we weren't there for her.

In the development of community you state your need, share it, and you hope everyone's wants do not collide or that there is not competition in neediness.

In 1991 and 1992 we were not there for all the needs.

Ill health invaded the group. Phyllis Chesler began to feel achy and fatigued and was diagnosed with Chronic Fatigue Immune Dysfunction Syndrome (CFIDS). For about six months Chesler had run a low-grade fever or had night chills or dizziness and disorientation and nausea. She suffered sleep disorders and became frightened as she realized that she was the only adult in her household and was not coping with this health emergency.

In Canada, Stephen Lewis, Michele Landsberg's husband, suffered the same symptoms. He, the golden-tongued orator of Canada, the political activist, was silenced for the months of recovery, lying inactive in his bed.

In mid-December 1991, Chesler wrote a single-spaced, five-page letter that she xeroxed and sent to the Seder Sisters as well as to her many other friends and acquaintances.

She wrote, "I am sure no one thought that I was living

alone, in great pain, and with no one to help me get through this. . . . For a variety of reasons, none malevolent, few people came to visit, few called."

We acknowledged the truth of that statement. We were all otherwise occupied with work, art, politics, family, and Brooklyn was far off from us Manhattan people, two or three trains away. Shamefully, we *were* negligent.

It made us all think, prodded by Chesler's letter, of those alone, without community or whom the community has neglected.

One of the Seder Sisters other than Chesler was feeling ill with prickly pain in the legs and was afraid of the genetic diabetes in the family that caused the amputation of her father's legs. She would awaken alone in her loft bed with her nightmares. And the Seder Sisters did little to alleviate her terrors. She had no health insurance, so what were her options in getting diagnosis?

While Stephen Lewis had access to the Canadian socialized health care, Phyllis did not.

What Chesler wanted, she stated in her letter, were "at least 10 to 15 people" and an ombudswoman to coordinate their activities on her behalf.

She wrote, "Neither individuals nor social institutions are prepared to take care of female adults—who are supposed to *be* the care givers."

She invited us to visit but could not promise us she'd be available, depending on health: "If you have a large, very quiet . . . place in the country, invite me. . . . Don't invite me if you expect energetic and sparkling conversation."

We Seder Sisters each reacted differently. Lilly invited Phyllis to come with Ariel and his school friend for a Shabbat dinner. Edith sent her love but also wrote of the people in her community who were alone and dying of AIDS. Bea brought a dinner to Brooklyn.

But we do not meet Phyllis's expectations.

The pre-planning session for the Seventeenth Seder is to be at Letty's. Phyllis faxes that she will not attend.

Lilly arrives unhappy, her hair crushed by her green hat.

"This is repetitive, this planning," she says. "We do it over and over, and what's to be gained from it?"

We are not family, she feels, maybe not even friends.

For some years now, Lilly has been feeling disillusioned.

"When things were good between us," she told me in an interview, "it was my community. It became my family.

"My mother had her first stroke some years ago around *Pesach*. I came back and was always so sad around *Pesach*. We always spoke our mothers' names and I always spoke of my mother with such pain. It was the only special place, at the seder, where I spoke about my pain. It took on more meaning—it was my family.

"The feminist seder was that blend of Jerusalem within me and my need for family. There was the excitement of the pre-planning, working with Esther and Phyllis. Phyllis was full of excitement: 'Rivlin! Come up with something.' I'd get going, sit at the typewriter. It was searching, challenging, beyond the daily. I thought I was part of something magical.

"It brought all aspects of my life together: feminist, need for family, and need for innovation. It comes from deep inside my roots and going beyond and doing holiday with women.

"I think about the year Letty talked about the difficulty of having leaders, how hard to accept our own leaders. Letty is very wise and she was wise that time.

"For me, I keep feeling it's over.

"There were years when the three of us did the creative stuff and they were very vital. We bounced off each other. I felt illuminated from some of those experiences. They were peak years. Just sitting here thinking about it thrills me, to be part of a growing *midrash*. I loved Miriam. I loved watching the *midrash* grow.

"It's over for me, and, even now, I'm crying. I'm mourning for it."

(Gloria has said about Lilly, "The experience was too important for her in the beginning and less important now than it should be.")

"I understand Chesler," says Rivlin. "We are both peripheral to the seder. We are single women and the rest of you have partners and we are alone, and we are not part of you."

Bea reminds Lilly, "We are all friends, for a long time now. But we also have other networks, other friends, all of us. We can't be everything for one another."

Lilly is unconvinced. "Maybe there should not be a seder. No more seders."

We are shocked. That alternative had never occurred to us.

Michele says, "I would be wounded. This is the closest I have to connection, to holiday, to ceremony. There is nothing like it in Toronto. I would be bereft without it."

Then Michele seeks compromise. "Maybe there should be a sabbatical."

Edith saves the day.

"What *would* be the theme just in case we decided to have a seder?" she asks.

Lilly thinks. "I am moved by the Russian women I've talked to who have come over. They say, 'There is a death of love in Russia.' That would interest me, the death of love."

Michele, of the body politic, is not interested in love as a prevailing theme. Gradually we suggest one thing, another.

"I met a wonderful woman today," says Letty, "who makes changes, a Black woman who changes the world around her. What about 'Change Makers?'"

"I love that!" says Lilly.

As for myself, I am leaving for Jerusalem immediately, to be gone for several months, even during the seder.

"How can we have the seder without you?" worries Michele.

How can they? I begin to worry also. Would someone else, I think possessively, don the yarmulke?

This is not a communal feeling.

When the Canadian film crew of *Weave of Women* brings me back in April for a fund-raiser, the sisters seem surprised. They had already begun the planning. Chesler offered to have the seder at her house. Lilly and Chesler were planning a way for the group to meditate, to relax, to sing between the speeches of the Change Makers. My return might be an inconvenience.

And I become ever more efficient, more organized, putting the Order of the Seder into my computer, as if that were an official edict.

That is community at odds.

Or odds and ends.

Not encompassing. Not willing to give over control.

"We will have to change," says Michele. "In the Autumn, I will fly in again from Toronto and we will have a long, thoughtful meeting—not hurriedly as we often do just before the seder. But leisurely, and we will talk about the community and what it needs and what we have to do to make it work."

A viable community negotiates. It is always in process, changing as the need arises.

Mostly, though, it has a shared vision and its members wish one another well.

Like a good marriage.

Or a loving partnership.

## PART SIX

Facts and Artifacts

Facts and Artifacts

PHYLLIS CHESLER understood that a stone can weep, an apple can feed a crowd, a spread can be a tent.

Objects are condensations of ritual: a wine cup, a mask, a bowl for the communal washing of hands. A fish chopper and wooden bowl puts the past between our hands. Songs are honey on the tongue.

The argument among the Seder Sisters has always been, do we teach or do we also listen to others? Do we give an audience the benefit of our experience, or do we attempt to include them? Inclusiveness has been our downfall, with many guests and their urgent stories. But how do we arrogate onto ourselves the right to be exclusive?

Here are the facts and references we used along the way on our journey.

1. THE WOMEN'S HAGGADAH

We sit in a circle, each with her own booklet, reading together. A group needs a written guide from which there can be excursions, preoccupations with other themes, and then return.

The written is always more formal than the spoken and more continuous. Each year we pick up *The Women's Haggadah,* alter it (as in the plagues), add to it (as in the matrilineage or the tales told), but we have something in the hand that allows us to be a congregation.

2. THE YARMULKE

The wearing of the yarmulke by women is of recent tradition, as is the wearing of the *talith,* prayer shawl. Women tired of pinning doilies on their head, looking like antimacassars. Perhaps out of respect for the proceedings, for those gathered, as well as for She Who Dwells in Our Midst, we cover our heads with the colorful Georgian, Bukharan yarmulkes or other festive headgear. Nothing is coerced.

3. THE CUP OF MIRIAM

We would see it tremble when we opened the apartment door, pressed the elevator button for Her ascension. The "Song to Miriam" we sing to the tune of *Elia-hu HaNavi,* the traditional song to the prophet Elijah.

4. THE SONGS

Aside from the poems in *The Women's Haggadah,* I would periodically write new lyrics. In 1985 we not only had a New Ten Commandments (Chesler et al.), but also new songs. As cantorial student Mikhal Schiff sang of our coming out of Egypt, we tried to see ourselves as if we went out of Egypt, joining hands with our sisters in the Black-Jewish New York Women's Dialogue Group. I was so pleased at this extending of our group that I wrote other new songs. It was a seder of outpouring.

I added verses to *Dayenu,* "It Would Have Been Sufficient."

In every group, something else suffices, and new verses must be written.

One could also alter the numbering songs. To "Who Knows One," for example, each guest might add her own counting. And for "One Kid, Only One Kid," *Had Gadya,* we think of all the tribal songs that go from the least to the most, from the kid to the Holy One.

To the song "It Happened at Midnight," *Oov'chen v'yehe bahetzi haleila,* I wrote, "She Could Not Sleep That Night," for different things keep women wakeful than men.

When we had our 1985 seder, New Commandments, New Songs Based Upon the Old, I added to *Dayenu:*

> If our fathers had not pitted our mothers against
> one another,
> like Abraham with Sarah and Hagar
> or Jacob with Leah and Rachel
> or Elkanah with Pnina and Hannah, *Dayenu.*
>
> If Sarah were understood to be a priestess, *Dayenu.*
>
> If Miriam were given her prophet's chair with
> Moses
> or her priesthood with Aaron, *Dayenu.*

For at least two seders we played tapes that honored our journey and that of our woman hero. One tape, mentioned before, *You Shall Be a Blessing,* is by Cantor Debbie Friedman. The lyrics are by the scholar Savina Teubal (author of *Sarah the Priestess* and *Hagar, the Egyptian*), based on Genesis 12:1–2. The song is *L'chi Lach.* Dr. Teubal's words and Cantor Friedman's music give women permission to cross borders, to join the journey, which is on the way to power and prayer.

Geela Razel Robinson Raphael has a bluegrass Miriam, with words and music on tape by *Rebel Maidels.*

We sang Geela's song:

> And Miriam took her timbrel out
> and all the women danced
> they danced, oh how they danced
> they danced the night away. . . .
> And Miriam took her timbrel out
> and all the women danced. . . .

"Bella," I once asked, "what more do we need at the seder?"

Bella said, "I think there should be a couple of written songs, reflecting our own psalms."

After all, many of our women heroes of the Hebrew Bible wrote songs: Deborah, the most ancient; Miriam; Judith's song. These were in the tradition of Near Eastern war chants.

Literature is derived from an oral, bardic tradition. We are the bards of our past, whether warlike or peaceful.

5. THE SACRED SCHMATA, TENT, SLAVE, APPLE, WATER, CORN

In the chapter, "The Symbolist," I discussed particular objects brought to us by Phyllis Chesler: the Sacred Schmata, the Tent, Apple of Eve, Corn of Joseph and Demeter, water from the well of Miriam.

I also mentioned elsewhere the iron double-mask designed by Susan Benton, with the opponents, Sarah and Hagar, front and back of the mask. Through Benton, these women of the Bible spoke in both of their voices and we felt the anger within the tent dissipate.

6. BOWLS, KNIVES, ONIONS, AND CREATURES

I have read of women's seders based upon *The Women's
Haggadah,* as printed in the April 1977 *Ms.* News photos
show women gathering, mothers and daughters making their
first seder together. The artifacts the mothers brought and
declared sacred are *their* mothers' wooden chopping bowls,
fish knives, and other implements for holiday making.
Family photographs were added by still other groups.

At a Los Angeles seder, using *The Women's Haggadah,*
Emily Levine, the Hollywood writer and stand-up comedi-
an, brought an onion.

"It's about unpeeling," said Emily Levine, "layers of our
history, of ourselves."

The onion was placed in the middle of the seder table,
alongside the horseradish, parsley, potato.

In 1988, a seder at the Canadian Mission, Phyllis suggested
we build a model. Lilly, the visualist, wanted photographs.
So, to a curious creature, begun with someone's mother's hat
affixed on top of a coat rack, were added beads, necklaces,
snapshots of our past. "She" stood in the corner, imperiously
hatted, regarding our ceremony.

We had a distinguished Conservative guest that year,
Francine Klagsbrun, who is one of those responsible for the
Jewish Theological Seminary finally opening its doors to
women rabbinical students. She looked somewhat worried at
the beginning of our seder, but by the time we were singing
L'chi Lach, she sang lustily along with the rest of us, paying
little or amused attention to the beaded, embellished creature
in the corner. Also with us was Anne Roiphe, whose own
memoir on regaining her Judaism encouraged Letty in her
pursuit.

7. WASHING THE HANDS

In the traditional Haggadah only the "head" of the household
washes *his* hands, twice. Here, we pass a bowl of water and
towel, rinse and wipe one another's hands. We service, tend
each other. We are all heads and hands of the household.

8. KITCHENWARE, OLD UTENSILS

We are, in part, what we and our mothers and grandmothers
used in the kitchen. Perhaps we have inherited an old
rebeisen, iron grater, or knife or pot.

Michele Landsberg said, "When I make a soup, I always use my grandmother's dented pot. It is part of the ritual."

9. DOCUMENTARIES

Like *Gefilte Fish,* a short documentary film on trying to follow the grandmother's recipe for making the fish, or many other current Jewish women's documentaries on their families, on searching their past, this might be a focus for the evening, tied in with the service. The established San Francisco Jewish Film Festival, the Boston Jewish Film Festival, and many others have shown current and old films. The filmmakers are frequently women, telling their seldom-told tales.

Says Lilly on the making of *Miriam's Daughters Now:* "I loved the Ninth Seder. I saw the opening of women's hearts, women sharing of their stories. . . . It made women sitting alone in isolated circumstances think there is a community. I was very happy that I chronicled this unique group of people that came together for a moment. I believe we were community."

10. MAKING SACRED SPACE

For our Ninth Women's Seder, Lilly and I came with our own tale of exodus and peace-making. We were in the Egyptian Sinai just a month before, hearing dialogue between Christians, Muslims, Native Americans, Sufis, Buddhists, Shintos. The purpose was, "To hear one another's tales and prayers."

"Give the heart a chance," said Joshua Mailman of the philanthropic organization Doughnuts, which sponsored this event. I mentioned previously that Chesler had rushed over from Brooklyn with the Schmata to give us added clout.

What do opponents or unfriendly neighbors or people unaware of others do together?

First we climbed Mount Sinai. We began at 2:00 AM in order to reach the top of the Mount at sunrise.

There, the Japanese greeted the rising sun, their symbol. Phillip Deere, a Native American, was smoking a peace pipe in the four directions of the earth. Two rabbis, Zalman Schachter and Marshall Meyer, sang *bruchot,* prayers, while another Jewish man blew the *shofar,* the ram's horn, from the mountain top. Pir Viliyat Khan, head of the Sufis, made a chorus of our voices as he directed our prayers into a braid that ascended upwards.

But, largely, women were absent. There may have been a woman Buddhist and a Christian woman or two. The women were absent from any ceremony.

As Lilly and I later described to the Seder Sisters, we called for a women's ceremony in the meeting tent. We were not given electricity but the women from the women's tent filled tin cans that had been left over from food with sand and stuck candles into them as our stage lights.

The tent filled with omans, mullahs, Copts, the Muslim Brotherhood people, the rabbis, as well as the women of every religion who were in the Sinai Gathering.

Lilly and I had prepared a script, and had asked for Egyptian and Israeli women volunteers.

I began, "In pharaonic time lived our ancestors Abraham and the women of his household."

Lilly and I told the familiar story, with new emphasis on the covenants God made with Hagar and with Sarah, telling each separately that she would be the mother of nations.

Lilly said, "As our mothers quarreled, their children and children's children have quarreled."

We had gathered Jewish-Israeli women and Egyptian women for this performance piece.

"Here are the daughters of Hagar and Sarah," we introduced them. "Let us question them. Let us hear their words."

We said further, "Daughters of Hagar: Rania and Jihan; Daughters of Sarah: Erika and Claudia, represented by a strip of sand, answer these questions."

The women sat facing one another, separated by the sand of the compound as the desert separated the two nations.

Lilly and I asked, "What do you see out of your windows? What causes you pain? What causes you pleasure? Who is close to your heart? What are your hopes for the future?"

The women saw their lives out of the window; they were close to their children or to God; they were pained by war; they were pleasured by love and they saw the future as their hopes for peace.

To make a covenant between them, the daughters of

Hagar and Sarah lit a candle in the desert and vowed not to bloody the sands with war.

Then Lilly and I took the Sacred Schmata out of its brown paper bag. We unwound it and tied it around the men and women standing in the Meeting Tent.

"You are now the witnesses," we told them.

From then on, during the Women's Seder, we never said the name *Egypt,* for those who bound the Israelites in slavery, but used the ancient name *Mitzraiim,* the narrow place.

Lilly and I told our Seder Sisters that we hoped we were in a broader place now.

That was the greatest adventure that befell the Sacred Schmata besides being rescued from a burning fire.

11. THE TABLE, THE TABLET

A table is everything from furniture, to a listing, to a slab. The Seder Sisters had the education of sitting around a table in dialogue.

Letty Cottin Pogrebin summoned us in 1985.

"It is time for Jewish and Black women to talk," she said, "to reconcile, to strengthen the women's movement, to act together and not separately."

Those of the Seder Sisters who met, some for two years, some longer, learned how to listen. We learned that there were buzzwords that instantly set each group off and kept us from listening and that we had to pause and explain those words.

The African-American women had urgent matters on their mind.

"The Black male is becoming an extinct species," one told us.

Another said, "I worry every time my young son goes out that he won't return."

We talked of drugs and jail. Law and order for the Jewish women was protection; for the African-Americans, it was a repressive force in their community hunting down the men and boys.

The African-Americans wearied of our speaking about the Holocaust. They felt they had had their own Holocaust, during the slave-shipping days, during slavery, and still it continued. What happened to the Jews was forty-five years ago, they said. For us, it was still current, an ever-present possibility. There was still ash in the air, we felt, ash on our clothing.

What eventually happened, out of goodwill, out of hurt, out of continuing to explain, was that our eyes met. Our eyes did not glaze or our ears wax over when the other spoke of that which discomforted us.

The meetings ended, I believe because our African-American sisters did not want a consciousness-raising group, a talk fest. Times were becoming desperate. And we Jewish women did not have a lot of power to effect change.

But it did lay the basis for working together. As each embarrassing and racist remark sprang from the city's then-mayor, we were determined to find a man of reconciliation to replace him. And, for that time, anyway, we did.

Our most intimate meeting was around the table at Bea's on Martin Luther King, Jr's, birthday. Betty Powell, academician, organizer, and with Kitchen Table Press, spoke of the importance of the church in her own past, instructing her to work for justice.

Lilly Rivlin spoke of the Zionist movement in teaching her about equality and justice and the possibility of a utopian society.

Amina Rahman, Black activist and administrator, then for the Board of Education and after for borough president and mayor David Dinkins, also spoke. It was the Civil Rights movement; it was SNCC, the Students Nonviolent Coordinating Committee, that raised her when she was a tough street kid, that housed her and gave her convictions.

The African-American women had attended our Women's Seder, and they discussed it at the next meeting of our dialogue group.

Betty Powell said, "It was your holiday and your territory and I felt summoned."

But in 1992, Betty Powell was honored as a Change Maker. Bea nominated her as a community worker, who educated the community about the interconnection between racism, anti-Semitism, and homophobia. Our meetings around the table taught us all.

12. NAME-CALLING, NAME-HONORING

Name calling—that reduction to a specific, to a denigra-
tive—is what we sometimes indulged in when we disagreed.

Bea called Lilly a *heterokopf,* someone who thinks in stereo-
typic heterosexual terms. During the Gulf War, Lilly called
pacifist Edith "Vanessa Redgrave."

I have also not been spared derogatives, from "manipula-
tive" to "benevolent dictator."

But we have also honored one another.

Merle Hoffman gave Chesler a Fiftieth Birthday, at Kate
Millett's loft. All of the women's movement showed up to
pay honor. It was more than a birthday. It was history.

We wore T-shirts, an Amazon riding a horse, with the let-
tering: Feminist Government in Exile.

That rider was Phyllis, galloping into the future.

The women, some years ago, proclaimed me Crone and
said that the words I uttered henceforth would be wise.

In April of '88, I thought of Letty as peacemaker and
wrote this to her:

> Who is she of wise counsel?
> The one who hears what is said,
>
> whether good or bad.
> The one who heeds it.
>
> The one who rises,
> who rises above it,
>
> turns it around,
> until, with sweet tongue,
>
> with wise words,
> she heals, and is proclaimed
> Medicine Woman of the Tribe.

We were one another's greatest critics and most rigorous
supporters.

13. WOMEN AT THE WALL

After our Healing Ceremony at Lilly's, which ended unsuc-
cessfully, several of us, Michele, Letty, Lilly, Phyllis, Bella,
and I, went to Jerusalem for the Empowerment of Women

conference. There something happened which stiffened our spines, our resolve. And one of us was especially affected for the next several years.

During the conference, the issue arose whether we wanted to have a service at the *Kotel,* the Western Wall. That is the outer wall of the Second Temple, built by Herod. Spiritually, it is a distance from a distance—the First Temple having been destroyed, then the Second Temple, and only the outer wall of the Second as evidence of its having been built. Since the War of '67 that united Jerusalem, the fundamentalists claimed this outer wall as their symbol and, gradually, with first a plastic partition, then granite boulders, turned it into the largest *mechitza,* separation, in the world. The men's side is about two-thirds of the wall. The women's side, only about a third, and bereft of the Torah. The women are not allowed to hold Bar or Bat Mitzvahs on their side. Even the voice raised in song is denied them.

We held a meeting at the conference, led by Rabbi Debby Brynn of Toronto, how to proceed. Every branch of Judaism was heard from at that discussion and each gave up something for the whole, to hold a prayer meeting with the Torah. The services would be *Halachic,* Orthodox, but we would be led by our women rabbis, from Reconstruction, Reform, and Conservative seminaries.

We rose early Thursday, December 1st, 1988, and boarded buses from the Hyatt Hotel, surreptitiously carrying the Torah. Fundamentalist men do not believe women should be allowed to touch the Torah or they would despoil it. Rabbi Helene Ferris had sequestered the Torah in her hotel room, having borrowed it from the Hebrew Union College. All night she thought she heard voices of those who would come and wrest the Torah from her.

Once on the square before the *Kotel,* we marched in a group to the women's side. We carried a folding table, set it up, unwrapped the Torah, and began our service.

The women wall guard realized what our singing meant and began pummelling us to get us to stop.

"The Torah belongs to men!" they shrieked.

Then, the *haredi,* the ultra-Orthodox, interrupted their praying, climbed on chairs to see over the *mechitza,* and commenced to bellow, to stick out their tongues at us, pulling down the sides of their mouths, shaking their fingers. They cursed us. They said, "I forbid it!" They said, "I excommunicate you!" They covered their eyes in horror at the sight of women praying together.

The *New York Times* had a still photographer there who photographed this body of women at the Wall, with the caption quoting from the Rabbi of the Wall, "Women with the Torah are like pigs at the *Kotel*."

In the meantime, Barry Purvis, Canadian cameraman, followed those of us who would be in the film, *Half the Kingdom*. When he heard our destination, he realized there would be drama. Purvis climbed the turret on the women's side where he had an overview of the whole episode, the only complete recording of what turned out to be an historic event that would eventually lead to the Israeli Supreme Court.

The women were given *aliyahs,* the honor of reading from the Torah. Phyllis Chesler was forever grateful to be chosen among the first readers.

The service having been completed, the seventy of us departed hurriedly but in a tight body. We were warned by the soldiers at the Wall that word had gone out to the *Yeshivoth,* the Orthodox Houses of Study, for the young men to come snatch away the Torah.

But we carried it with dignity back to the Hyatt, where, mission accomplished, we felt like warriors. We did not know that was only the beginning of the battle.

From then on, every week Israeli women came with the Torah, in a group, to greet the Sabbath, and every week they were reviled, chairs were thrown at them, their hair pulled. But they continued to sing.

In the States, a group forms around Phyllis Chesler and Rivka Haut in support of Women at the Wall. Amazon and Orthodox are a powerful mixture.

Words of Mothers and Others

ONE MAKES CHOICES in putting on an event such as a Women's Seder.

You may have a consistent leader or alternating leaders. If the group is a collective, you may take turns conceiving the seder. Or, one need not have leaders at all, which creates yet a different kind of seder.

How do the Seder Sisters feel about the process of these past seventeen years?

Letty has said, "When the seder happens, it is always satisfying and magical. . . . We go wrong when we let egomaniacal needs take over."

Why does this happen?

Letty answers, "The ceremony creates a place for quarrels of honor. It is an empty throne where someone sits. In a way it is a paradigm for an exclusively female structure, not enough slots in the seder."

But she has written, in *Deborah, Golda, and Me,*

> On this night [of the Women's Seder], we become ourselves. We speak with grammar of the feminine plural and invoke the Shechina. . . . On this night we give [woman's] story equal time.

And, after our Healing Ceremony, she wrote about contention in *Lilith,* Spring '89.

> Instead of hiding our disputes, I believe we must air them. Instead of feminine conformity, I believe in passionate advocacy. Our arguments are not petty outbursts ruled by personality or ego; they are meaningful expressions of diverse values and strategies.

No "feminine conformity" for us!

Gloria feels, "This should be the drop-off to start other

groups." She wants "a chosen family" and a new kind of community. She has a different center, in the apartment and in her sense of self.

She is a Seder Mother, but also a Solstice Sister. She continues to come to the Women's Seder and, also, has a "drop-off group." On the nights of the Solstices and Equinoxes, she meets with the "Solstice Sisters," who gather, not to attach themselves to history or to a people, but to hear one another deeply, to ask for help, and then, wickedly, playfully, with eagle feathers and plastic wands, tap each other on the head and say, "Do it! You'll do it!"

Grace Paley has said, again, "I loved the process. As long as people think they are discovering something and work toward it and are trying to understand our relationship as Jewish women to the history and life of our people, [the Women's Seder is] a wonderful thing and should go on.

"If the seder doesn't go on, I would feel bad. I want to be asked next time. But it's very possible it should be reorganized. Have two Women's Seders."

Michele says, "At the seder I feel we're like pioneers, invading, claiming our territory.

"To me, the wounds of outrage and insulted womanness go so deep, what I suffered as a child, and the wounds of Jewishness. This was the reverse side of the wounds—a glorying. I felt strong and overweening. . . . I allowed myself to overween a bit.

"The artistic work was the thing that so impressed me and made it all so valuable. To work and create with poetry, language, and insight and to make it beautiful, that made it real to me."

She summarizes some of us: "Chesler is oracular. Power storms are her domain. Broner presides by grace of artistry. Bea and Edith hold forth with necessary skepticism. I felt it was all graceful.

"The seder is always a burden, but it's always beautiful when it happens and it's always worth it. I hope I'll always be at the seder. The lore is spreading even in Canada.

"I was amazed how tolerantly the group accepted conflict. No one has been excluded. That truly is feminism, not to exclude someone because of the bad as well as the good."

Here one thinks of Lilly's summary of good parts, *maalot,* and bad parts, *heser henanot,* virtues and vices in the group.

Michele smiles. "I couldn't be that tolerant, but the group has resources beyond its individual members."

With Lilly, what pleased her the most these years was "taking my roots and going beyond. . . . No other experience did it so completely. . . . Just sitting here thinking about it thrills me, to be part of a growing *midrash."*

But Lilly has a conflicting thought. "We were such a paradigm for others and what did we do? Paradise Lost."

Bella thinks about the seders and that they helped her to feel.

"I was trained as an intellectual. I've learned to overcome it and become intuitive."

Her best friend, Shirley MacLaine, also helps her in this process.

"Shirley MacLaine says that when you make a speech or take a political action, you not only deal with the dialectic of your speech but also with a feeling of great love and hope, rather than coming from anger or from just putting a bunch of facts together and spinning them out."

Bella thinks of her other friends.

"Gloria Steinem is a very good friend, and we spent a lot of time being soul mates about the growing women's movement. We've maintained a closeness, but it's not as daily as it used to be."

As for the seder, "The Women's Seder delves into the soul of womanhood. Very challenging, almost like people making confessions. It's spiritual, like an opening up of human history and placing a different heart and a different soul in it. It captures my emotions, but I guess they were there all along.

"I look forward to it every year. I was supposed to do something Sunday [of the seder] and I wouldn't go. [The Women's Seder is] an important spiritual movement, healing, and also I'm shocked to hear what I have said and to hear other people. It's so beautiful to be able to share people's emotions. In the arenas in which I function, people don't do that."

As for daughters, "I want my daughters *there* but they're not as engaged in the tradition the same way I am. That is the way of daughters. But they *are* engaged in searching for the spirit of woman."

She thinks about the Daughters' Seder. "Still a purity. They were pure. They haven't gone through the grinding wheels of conflict. It was in some ways more restrained, more inhibited, but it had unexpected depths and it was respectful."

And the future of the seders? "I feel that we have to change the focus. The time has come to try and analyze women in the biblical history of the time and subsequently. It would be appropriate."

What do we want from our seders?

In the words of our Seder Mothers and Sisters, feeling, artistry, searching, and "unexpected depths," and, even, something "respectful."

For our Eighteenth Seder, we will either have a large hall or an intimate space or both. We will talk it through, disagree, and then agree. We have set a pattern for negotiation—as well as for pleasure, joy, and ritual—through community.

◆　◆　◆　◆

CALIFORNIA, APRIL, 1992

I am about to return to Israel for the rest of my stay. Before I do, I visit my family in San Francisco.

My family is planning for Passover. Adam buys five three-hundred pound bags of sand. He turns a room into a desert. He makes a tent of bedsheets. He puts drawing paper on the walls, and draws the moon as seen from the tent, sheep peering in. His little son Emmanuel thinks Passover happens in a sandbox.

I visit my other children to ask for their help on this project.

"What is the book?" I ask my son Jeremy. "What should *The Telling* be?"

Jeremy has been helping me to shop for a laptop computer in the Bay Area.

"The book is the group. The book is about the group being together and how it has affected their lives," he says. "It should be cyclical, circular."

He strokes his dark beard.

"If you get a lot of high-powered women together, though, who have been fighting for what they believe in all their lives, they will continue to fight."

"That's not all the book," I say.

The laptops are too numerous and confusing. We sit in his van and talk.

"The seder has been wandering in the desert," says Jeremy. "There is a discernible journey. The members of the seder might come to say, 'We are changed and we are changing.'"

He delivers me to his sister.

"What is the book?" I ask Sari.

Sari, the traveler, has settled. She writes about her being a wanderer in *Everything Is Real Except the Obvious* (Mill Valley CA: EM Press, 1992):

> I was born on the East Coast, raised in the Midwest. Despite a vague sense of direction, I travelled to the Near, Middle, Far East and Down Under. I now live with my husband, Milton Kalish, in the Far West. The movement is as mysterious to me as the sudden flight of blackbirds upward into the branches of a tree. A secret message, the desire for a better view?

I knew I would get direction from her.

"What is the book about?" I ask Sari.

She instantly takes out a purple pen to write on a purple pad.

"Teaching people how to make ritual" is the topic sentence, then, "Chapters organized by theme."

Sari believes we need a recipe or a spell, a list of props, and a ritual around a particular theme.

"You need a description of the events in a year that the ritual addressed," she writes, "to set the story. Make it 'reporting' or 'play.' Have your characters speak as if onstage."

She then proceeds to show me her Blessing Box filled with such spirit, hope, and poetry that I want to kiss it with my fingertips.

I take son's and daughter's advice with me and follow it closely.

◆ ◆ ◆ ◆

JERUSALEM, JUNE, 1992

The biblical is the reference for both the spiritual and political.

It is ten years since the invasion of Lebanon. Women in Black, a group that has worn black and stood in opposition to the occupation of the Territories, has invited others to stand vigil with them.

One young man holds a sign that says, "'The voice of my bother's blood cries unto me from the earth,' General Sharon." He is quoting from Genesis 4:9, the murder of Abel by Cain. Perhaps the young man lost his brother; perhaps the Lebanese are his brothers. But he hears the voices of the dead crying from the earth.

The birds rise and sing *sachrit,* the morning prayers, we're told. The sun rises at *Ayelit haShachar,* the deer of dawn.

A potter, Raya Redlich, takes us to Sherover Promenade. There she speaks of messengers from "The Other Side."

"What do you mean?" I ask.

"When someone has died, I receive a messenger. Twice it was from a ladybug."

"Why a ladybug?" I ask.

"It's good luck here and, also, it has a curious name. In Hebrew it's called *parat Moshe rabanu,* 'the calf of Moses, our teacher.' It's a messenger. Each time, the ladybug let me know there had been a death."

"Really?" I ask.

"I called a zoologist and asked, 'Do you ever receive messages from the Other Side through insects or animals?' And he said, 'Yes, I do.'"

In the Sherover Promenade, a ladybug falls on Raya's hand. She looks at it fondly and questioningly before she brushes it off.

"No messages."

◆ ◆ ◆ ◆

Nomi Nimrod and Haggai come for an overnight visit. It is their first time alone with each other in seventeen years, since the first of their four daughters was born. They have been living in kibbutzim, raising their daughters communally. Haggai teaches Hebrew literature and Nomi teaches writing.

They bring three presents: a photograph of four smiling girls; a new Hebrew version of our songs, "Song of Sources," "It Happened at Midnight," and "Dayenu," and a book. The book is most appropriate, *The Miracle Hater*, by the Jerusalem writer Shulamith Hareven (trans. Hillel Halkin, San Francisco: North Point Press, 1988).

"She could have been in the room with us while we were writing," says Nomi. "The book is a new interpretation of the Exodus legend."

Exodus is always with us, whether in or out of the land.

◆   ◆   ◆   ◆

At Shabbat dinner, Alice Shalvi, head of the Women's Network in Israel, tells us that the harvest is ready, the corn light gold in the hills. Along the highways one can see the barley being harvested, as in the book of Ruth. This is *Shavuoth,* where one reads from the book of Ruth.

Gloria Steinem said, "I am Gloria, the daughter of Ruth, the daughter of Ruth. My mother told me of the book of Ruth and said, 'A woman said that to another woman— Wither thou goest I will go; and where thou lodgest, I will lodge—instead of to a man.'"

It's the only such story in the Hebrew Bible.

At the end of the month I return to my Sisters, for where they go, I will go, and where they dwell, there will I dwell. And we will celebrate together.

The Women's Haggadah

By E. M. Broner and Naomi Nimrod
Revised 1992, by E. M. Broner

FILL the first cup of wine.

Say, "Here am I prepared to observe the mitzvah of drinking the four cups of wine for the sake of the Shekhinah, Blessed be She."

THIS IS THE FIRST CUP OF WINE.

We drink the first cup, saying, "We return to Egypt."

THE FOUR QUESTIONS OF WOMEN

◆ **Why is this Haggadah different from traditional Haggadoth?**
Because this Haggadah deals with the exodus of women.

◆ **Why have our Mothers on this night been bitter?**
Because they did the preparation but not the ritual. They did the serving but not the conducting. They read of their fathers but not of their mothers.

◆ **Why on this night do we dip twice?**
Because of the natural and unnatural cycles of blood: our monthly bleedings; the blood spilled by war.

◆ **Why on this night do we recline?**
We recline on this night for the unhurried telling of the legacy of Miriam.

WE WERE SLAVES unto Pharoah in Egypt. And the Shekhinah brought us from there with a mighty hand and outstretched arm. If the Holy One had not brought out our daughters and sons, our children's children, we would still have been slaves to Pharoah in Egypt. Although if were all wise, all sensible, experienced, understanding of the Torah, it would still be our duty to tell of the departure from Egypt, and the more one tells of the departure from Egypt, the more she is to be praised.

IT IS SAID that four women gathered in Bnai Barak, reclining on cushions and relating the Exodus from Egypt. They are our foremothers: Rachel, Beruriah, Ima Shalom, who was a descendent from the house of Hillel, and her niece, the daughter of Rabbi Gamliel.

Our mothers spent that Night of Vigil relearning their history until their daughters came to them and said, "Mothers, the time has come to say the morning *schma.*"

THE FOUR DAUGHTERS
Through four daughters we shall learn the Torah of Departure. Four daughters and their mothers spent this Night of Vigil seeing themselves as if they went out of Egypt. From Egypt they went out, but not from the house of bondage.

Four questions were asked and four answers were given.

THE SONG OF SEARCHING
Why is this night both bitter and sweet?
The story of women is bitter. The search-
ing together is sweet.

Why do we dip into the wine of history?
We were led out of Egypt
by the jingle of timbrel,
the echo of song.

What still plagues us in our chronology?
The pestilence of tradition,
the affliction of custom,
the calamity of rabbinic decree.

When shall we lean back comfortably?
We shall not recline
until we find our dignity.

Four daughters arrive, one wise, one wicked, one simple, and one who does not know how to question.

THE WISE ONE, what does she say: "Mothers, what did the Shekhinah command of you that you sit here all this night and talk of departures?"

THE WICKED ONE, what does she say: "Why are you sitting here all the night, only you women? Women have nothing to say to one another. Women have nothing to learn from one another."

By her saying this she removes herself from the community of women and isolates herself.

The elderly women tell her, "You have broken the chain that links you to our heritage and to the legacy of Miriam. You are still in the house of bondage."

THE SIMPLE ONE, what does she say? "What is this?" She is referring to the inheritance from Miriam. The older women relate to her the legends in the *Haggadah* about the first prophet.

THE ONE THAT DOES NOT KNOW HOW TO QUESTION, for her the others must open the way.

The first mother, Rachel, begins. Rachel, the daughter of a wealthy family, married the shepherd of the household. For this she was disinherited. In spite of her poverty, she sent her husband far away to learn Torah.

Rachel tells of Miriam:

"This legend was told by Rabbi Yehuda bar Zevena. Amram, the father of Miriam, was great in his generation. When he heard Pharoah proclaim, 'All the sons that are born, ye shall cast into the Nile,' Amram said, 'We are toiling in vain.' Amram divorced his wife and the people, following his example, also divorced their wives.

"His daughter Miriam said to her father, 'You condemned us more than Pharoah because he only condemned the males but you condemned males and females. What Pharoah decreed was only for this world, but your decree is for this and the next world.

'Pharoah is a villain so there is doubt about whether his decree will be fulfilled, but you are a just man so it is sure that your decree will be obeyed.'

"Amram listened to his daughter and took back his wife, Yocheved. All of his followers remarried their wives. The child Miriam and her brother Aaron sang and danced at the ceremony."

Beruriah continues with the narration. Beruriah's wisdom is known far and wide and she is praised in Talmudic literature.

"When Miriam was five her mother was pregnant with Moses. Miriam prophesied, 'My mother is about to bear a son who will save Israel from Egypt.'

"On the day Moses was born, the house was filled with light. Her father Amram kissed Miriam on the head and said, 'Your prophecy was fulfilled.'

"Three months later her brother was put into a basket and set floating on the Nile.

"Her father hit her on the head and asked, 'Daughter, now where is your prophecy?'

"That is why it is said in the Hebrew Bible, 'The child's sister took her stand at a distance to see what would happen to him.' (Exodus 2:4)

"She was the first of all prophets. Why was she given the name Miriam? 'Mar' is bitter, for it was a bitter time. 'Mari' is rebellion, for the Jews expressed their bitterness in rebellion."

Ima Shalom, the third mother, received an education befitting the sister of a "nasi," a leader, and the daughter of Hillel the Great.

IMA SHALOM SAYS : "Listen, my daughters, to the story of Miriam. When the time came for Yocheved to

give birth, Miriam shared her mother's travails. She pre-
dicted Moses; she saved Moses and she saw to it that he
was nursed by his own mother while in the house of
Pharoah. On the night when she and Yocheved put
Moses into the water, Miriam, the child, grew up.

"When, years later, it was time for the exodus,
Miriam sang and danced her people to victory. The
house of Israel sang a song of freedom to the sound of
Miriam's tambourine. The women gathered around her
and they mocked those who cried: 'Leave us alone! Let
us be slaves to the Egyptians. We would rather be slaves
to the Egyptians than die here in the Wilderness.'"
(Exodus 14:12–13)

> **THE SONG IN THE WILDERNESS**
> **We will be slaves to no nation and before
> no man.**
> **We can find our way through the wilder-
> ness.**
> **We can find our way through thicket and
> stone.**
> **We can find our way under hot desert sun
> to our home.**

IMA SHALOM CONTINUES: "It is said in the
Haggadah that after the children of Israel crossed the
Red Sea, they burst into song. When the Prophet
Miriam sang, legends goes, the child on the knee and
the suckling baby saw the Shekhinah. The suckling
baby let go of the breast and started to sing and the child
on the knee lifted its voice in prayer. Even the embryos
heard singing from the wombs of their mothers."

> **THE SONG OF QUESTIONS**
> **Mother, asks the clever daughter,**
> **who are our mothers?**
> **who are our ancestors?**
> **what is our history?**
> **Give us our name. Name our genealogy.**

Mother, asks the wicked daughter,
if I learn my history, will I not be angry?
Will I not be bitter as Miriam
who was deprived of her prophecy?

Mother, asks the simple daughter,
if Miriam lies buried in sand,
why must we dig up those bones?
Why must we remove her from the sun
   and stone
where she belongs?

The one who knows not how to question,
she has no past, she has no present, she
   can have no future
without knowing her mothers,
without knowing her angers,
without knowing her questions.

THE DAUGHTER OF RABBI GAMLIEL, who
has suffered in her own life, says: "There is anger in our
heritage. In the desert Miriam and Aaron asked, 'Is
Moses the only one with whom the Lord has spoken?
Has He not spoken with us as well?' The Lord passed
among them and left Miriam white with leprosy but
Aaron unharmed. Miriam was treated like the wicked
daughter whose father spat in her face and sent her from
the tent for seven days until she was forgiven."

THE LAMENT OF THE PROPHET MIRIAM
Once she danced at the banks of the sea.
Once the women leapt after her.
Then she praised the One on High
and her tambourine rose in the air.

And the rain in the wilderness
tasted like coriander,
like almond and honey,
but the taste in her mouth was "Maror,"
bitter as her name.

"You shall be a Kingdom of Priests."
She was not appointed.
"And a land of prophets."
She was not heeded.
"Come up unto the Lord,"
Moses, Aaron, and Seventy Elders.
"Come up unto the Lord,"
Joshua.
"Come up to me into the Mount,
and the Lord spoke unto Moses
and the Lord spoke unto Moses
and the Lord said unto Moses . . .
Moreover, the Lord spoke unto Moses.
And He gave unto Moses . . .
Moreover the Lord spoke with Moses
and He gave unto Moses
two tablets of stone.
Come up unto the Lord
Come up to me unto the Mount
And take Aaron and his sons."

"And the Lord spoke
and Moses . . . the skin of his face shone."
"And the Lord spoke with Moses and
  Aaron
and the Lord spoke with Moses
in Mount Sinai."
"And the Lord spoke with Moses
in the wilderness of the Sinai."

"And Miriam and Aaron spoke against
  Moses."
Miriam's face did not shine.
"Behold: Miriam became leprous,
white as snow."
  Pale in the wilderness
  for the counting of seven days,
  shut out from the camp,
  tented in dishonor.

Soon, she lay herself down,
the sister of Moses,
the prophet of her people,
she lay down
in a place of no seed, no fig,
no wine, no pomegranate,
no water,
and, parched, Miriam died.

THE DAUGHTER OF RABBI GAMLIEL SAYS:
"When Miriam died, Moses and Aaron prepared her for
burial. It is said that she died with a kiss from the
Shekhinah, for the Angel of Death could not take her.

"As Moses brought Joseph's bones out of Egypt, so,
Miriam, we will bring your bones out of Kadesh, out of
the desert."

THE DAUGHTERS ASK, "How did it come about
that Miriam was treated so badly?"

"That has to do with the legend of our origins," say
the mothers.

SONG OF OUR SOURCES
We were created together,
the man and the woman,
not one from the other,
not one the helper,
the other the master.
We were created together
for ourselves and each other.

But the rabbis all agree
that woman was created last,
that woman was created least.

Adam was all alone,
jealous of the birds in heaven,
of the reptiles mating on earth,
of the fish in the water,
of the fruit trees in the garden.

The rabbis all agree
that woman was created last,
that woman was created least.

So Adam was given
something a little more
than a bird that sang in heaven,
a creature that crawled on the earth,
a thing that swam in the water.

The rabbis all agree
that woman was created last,
that woman was created least.

She was not made from the head
they said
lest she hold herself too high.
She was not made from the eyes
they said
lest she peer into the sky.

The priests all agree. . . .

She was not made from the ear
for think of the voices she'd hear.
She was not made from the heart
or she would be painfully hurt.

The priests all agree. . . .

She was not made from the hand
or she'd touch everything in the land.
She was not made from the mouth
or soon you would hear her shout.

The ministers all agree. . . .

She was made only from the rib
to do as she was bid.
She was made only from the rib
to do as she was bid.

The ministers all agree.

The men of God agree
that Eve was weak,
that Eve was sinful
that God on the same day
made Eve and Evil.

The rabbis all agree. . . .

These men they agree,
but I cannot agree.
My mother was a woman.
My mother was human.
She spoke, heard, touched, felt.
I sing bitterly in this song
that the men of God were wrong.

ORIGINALLY OUR FOREMOTHERS and fore-
fathers were worshipers of gods and goddesses and they
dwelt on the other side of the river from time immemorial
until the Shekhinah came. The Shekhinah took Abraham
and Sarah from the other side of the river and walked
them throughout the land of Canaan. The womb of Sarah
was fertilized by the seed of Abraham and they bore Isaac.
In order to continue the line, the cousins, Rebecca and
Isaac, bore the twins Jacob and Esau. To Esau and to all of
his household—to his wives, daughters, sons, the
Shekhinah gave Har Seir, even to the wives Ada, the
Hittite, Ahalevama, whose mother was Ana, to Esau's
cousin, Basmot, daughter of his uncle Ishmael, and to all
of the other women who came unto Har Seir to inherit it.

THE FIRST EXODUS, that of Jacob, Leah, Rachel,
Bilha, Zilpa and all their household, is the exodus of one
family, and it takes place within a generation. The second exodus, from Egypt, is of the tribes of Israel, descendants of the house of Sarah and Abraham, whose people
dwelled there over four hundred years.

THEY WENT DOWN INTO EGYPT, the descendants of our mothers: Sarah, Rebecca, Rachel, Leah, Bilha, that bore Naptali, and Zilpa, that bore Asher. They came to Egypt, Jacob and all his descendants with him, his sons and their sons, his daughter and his sons' daughters.

Who of our mothers went down into Egypt?

Rachel died in childbirth in Bet Lecham. Leah is buried in the cave of Machpelah. Leah's daughter Dina was buried by her brother Simeon in Canaan. Serach, granddaughter of Zilpah and Jacob, is the only woman named among the seventy that went down to Egypt.

THE COVENANT WITH ISRAEL begins with the promise to Sarah and Abraham that they would not be without off-spring, that their daughters and sons would leave Canaan, would sojourn in a land not theirs, would do hard labor for four hundred years. Afterwards they would go out with great riches from Egypt and return to Canaan.

V'HE SH'AMDA—THE PROMISE
And this promise has supported our foremothers, our forefathers and ourselves, for not only one has risen up against us but in every generation some have arisen against us to annihilate us but the Holy One saved us from their hands.

V'HE SH'LO AMDA—THE PROMISE NOT KEPT
And what is the promise to women? That we have effect on our own lives and the generations that follow us.

In every generation we lost our names and our legacy.

Our role became fertilization of the generations of men.

Our foremothers died and were buried after fulfilling this purpose.

In every generation there have arisen against us those who would destroy us and we have not yet been delivered from their hand.

LIFT the second cup.
THIS IS THE SECOND CUP OF WINE.
We drink the second cup, saying, "We return to
the desert."

"Who would rise against our mothers?" asks the
Simple Daughter.
"The family and the state," is the answer.

THE STOLEN LEGACY

BERURIAH was known for her *midrashim,* commen-
taries on the law. She guided her husband, Rabbi Meir,
in correct interpretation. When Rabbi Meir was upset
by the unruly behavior of the people in his section of
the city, he prayed for their death: "Let the wicked be
no more."

Beruriah said, "In Psalm 104 it says *sins* and not *sinners.*
You must pray for mercy towards the people and for the
death of the sin."

He did as she suggested.

Beruriah was to have arguments of more serious con-
sequences with her husband later.

Beruriah was infuriated by the attitude of the rabbis
towards women. Her conversation with Rabbi Jose
Galilee is typical of her sharp wit.

Rabbi Jose Galilee was walking on his way. Beruriah
crossed his path. He said to her, "What way should I
go to the town of Lod?" She replied, "Galilee—Stupid!
Did not our wise men say, 'You should not talk at
length with women'? Galilee, you should have asked,
'How to Lod?'"

Beruriah will die before her time and will not con-
duct more seders. She will die because of jealousy on
the part of her husband and the humiliating test he
put to her.

Rabbi Meir said to Beruriah, "Women are light-
minded." When she objected her husband warned her
that her own end might testify to the truth of his words.
Putting her virtue to the test, Rabbi Meir charged one

of his students to endeavor to seduce her. After repeated efforts on the student's part, Beruriah yielded. Shame, it is said, drove her to suicide. It is also said that she lies buried on the other side of the cemetery wall.

Which leads one to two questions.

Ima Shalom asks, "Who are the guilty? The woman who yields to temptation, or the man who created the situation in order to test her? Beruriah was dishonored in death, but no dishonor befell her husband or seducer."

The niece of Ima Shalom asks, "And, why would such an unlikely story of a virtuous and learned woman be told?"

"Because women's learning is anathema. If women read books, soon they will write books. And the heroes and plots will change. If women read Torah, they will write the unsung songs, and name the nameless women."

IMA SHALOM SAYS, "I learned in the house of the father of my father and was called upon for advice in the house of my husband, Rabbi Eliezer ben Hyrcannus. And yet it was he who said to our son, 'It is better to burn the words of the Torah than to give them to women.'"

RACHEL is the daughter of Kalba Shavuah, a wealthy man. While living in her father's house she noticed a modest but good shepherd. Rachel proposed marriage to this shepherd on the condition that he go to the House of Learning to study Torah. When Rachel's father learned of this unsuitable match, he disinherited his strong-willed daughter and threw her out of the house.

AKIVA and Rachel moved into a hut and slept on straw. Each morning Akiva would remove blades of straw from his bride's hair. Rachel reminded Akiva of his promise to study in the *Beth Midrash* where she, a woman, would not be allowed. Akiva kept his word and left his wife. Rachel cut her hair and sold the braids to send him money for his studies.

There are stories that Akiva studied for twelve years. Some say it was for twice that and another legend says that it was for forty years. Rachel continued to live poorly.

When Akiva returned as a great men with twelve thousand students attending him, Rachel, a ragged old woman, approached. His students shoved her away. Akiva then recognized his wife and said to his students, "Do not prevent her from coming to me for what is mine and yours is hers."

THE SIMPLE DAUGHTER ASKS, "Is there a husband who sends his wife to study for forty years, twenty-four or even for twelve, and lives in poverty to maintain her?"

The mothers answer, "Such has not been the custom."

THE NIECE OF IMA SHALOM, DAUGHTER OF RABBI GAMLIEL. SHE HAS NO GIVEN NAME: "My father thought I was clever. He respected the answers I gave to an unbeliever.

"When I married and came to him twice for his blessings, this is what he said: 'Let it be that you should not return here.' When I bore a male son, he said to me, 'Let it be that you should never cease from crying, Alas!'

"When I told him, 'Two times happiness came to me and each time you cursed me,' he replied, 'Both curses are blessings. Because I want you to have peace in your home, you should not return here. Because I want your son to live, Alas! shall not cease from utterance from your lips. Alas that my son did not eat! Alas that my son did not drink! Alas that my son did not go to the synagogue.'

"My father no longer remembers me or my learning."

> SONG OF THE MOTHERS
> **Years ago in Bnai Barak**
> **four women learned this saying:**
> **'Because of Just Women**
> **Israel is redeemed from Egypt.'**
>
> **Shiphrah, Puah, brave women,**
> **midwifed a nation**

by disobeying Pharaoh.
The children were born
in rebellion.

But not in the sources
were Just Women rewarded.
Miriam died in obscurity.

Four women on the Night of Vigil
learn of the anger of women.
Though her knowledge of Torah be great,
the story of Beruriah is a lesson
that one can be expelled again
for eating of the tree of knowledge.

Ima Shalom, from the House of Hillel,
guided her husband Eliezer to wisdom.
Instead of praise, he heaped scorn:
"If Torah be given a woman,
better let it be burned."

Rachel, a reader of Torah,
was disinherited,
for choosing knowledge and love.
In poverty with her shepherd she slept,
straw and hay in her hair and bed.
Because she could not learn,
she sent him to learn in her stead
and he studied for forty years,
while she slept on a hard pallet
and chewed hard crusts of bread.

The daughter of Rabbi Gamliel
went the natural course of women
but her father's blessings were curses.
She cried a heaving last, Alas!
In which all the bitterness
of learned women
was expressed.

LIFT the third cup.
THIS IS THE THIRD CUP OF WINE.
*We drink the third cup, saying, "I drink to the dregs
the cup of knowledge."*

THE SIMPLE DAUGHTER ASKS the Mothers,
"Is there more to be learned?"
    "We have to learn of our plagues," says Ima Shalom.
    "And of what suffices," says Beruriah.
    "And for whom to open the door," says Rachel.

THE PLAGUES OF WOMEN

1. Blood
> The bleeding and bearing cycle of the
> female
> is considered unclean by the male.
> She will be killed,
> her blood spilled
> if holy places, priests and men
> are approached by bleeding women.
> And so woman is forcibly removed
> from power and rule because of blood.

    The Tribal Council of Men Did Not Listen to the
Voices of Women.

2. The Frog: False Self-Image
> A constant froggy smile,
> fear of the frown,
> the raised voice or hand,
> she hops into the house,
> to the bed chambers,
> falls into pots, ovens,
> the kneading trough.
> She has squatted so long,
> she has no size.

3. Lice: Dissatisfied
   She scratches her life
   like a lice-filled head.

4. The Gnat: Unknown
   She fills the eyes with dark spots,
   the ears with buzzing dust.
   Yet, though she is a multitude,
   she is invisible,
   though she is a pestilence,
   unnameable.

5. Noxious Beasts
   Those who beat her,
   ostracize her,
   brutalize, make vermin of her,
   then fertilize her.

6. Boils: Jealousy
   It is recognized in Numbers
   that man will be jealous of woman.
   There is a grain offering
   he comes bearing.
   The priest becomes his tool
   and issues a priestly rule
   that woman must prove she is sinless
   but man is always guiltless.
   Before the whole community
   man is given authority over woman's
   body
   and the issue of her womb.
   But for woman's feelings
   there is neither hearing nor room.

And the Tribal Council Hardened Its Heart Against
Women.

7. Moraine: Woman as Sinful
>Solomon the Ruler said,
>"The wiles of women
>are more bitter than death.
>Her heart is a trap to catch you.
>Her arms are fetters
>to make man a sinner.
>Only by grace of God
>can we ever escape her."

8. Locusts: Legal Discrimination
>The generations are figured
>from father to son
>and thus woman
>depends upon man
>for he is her legal guardian.
>She can keep no obligation,
>promise or vow
>that man cannot disallow.
>Because she was by the serpent beguiled
>she can never be legally more than a
>child.

9. Darkness
>It became pitch-dark
>in the history of women.
>They could not see one another.
>And none stirred from where she sat.
>All lights of learning were dimmed
>and the doors of the House of Study were
>locked.
>The woman could not read.
>The woman could not write,
>could not take part in her community,
>could not participate
>in writing her own history.

And the Tribal Council Abandoned the Women.

10. Slaying of the Spirit

> It happened that first midnight
> when he passed over her
> and she bowed her head and worshiped.
> With all women it was thus,
> from the highborn to the lowly,
> they became captive spirits.
> And no one heard them cry,
> yet, in each house, had the women
> expired.

AND THE TRIBAL COUNCIL NEVER LET THE HEBREW WOMEN GO OUT OF BONDAGE.

"But what is 'dayenu,' what is sufficient for us?" asks the Wise Daughter.

DAYENU

> If Eve had been created in the image of
> God
> and not as helper to Adam,
> it would have sufficed.
> *Dayenu.*
>
> If she had been created as Adam's equal
> and not as temptress,
> *Dayenu.*
>
> If she were the first woman to eat
> from the Tree of Knowledge,
> who brought learning to us,
> *Dayenu.*
>
> If Sarah were recognized as a priestess,
> royal in her own lineage,
> *Dayenu.*

If Lot's wife had been honored and not
mocked
when she turned her head
as devastation befell her children,
and not mocked for the falling
and freezing of her tears,
Dayenu.

If our foremothers had not been
considered
as hardened roots
or fruit-bearing wombs,
but as women in themselves,
Dayenu.

If our fathers had not pitted our mothers
against each other,
like Abraham with Sarah and Hagar
or Jacob with Leah and Rachel
or Elkanah with Hannah and Pnina,
Dayenu.

If Miriam were given her prophet's chair
or the priesthood,
Dayenu.

If the Just Women in Egypt
who caused our redemption
had been given sufficient recognition,
Dayenu.

If women bonding, like Naomi and Ruth,
were the tradition
and not the exception,
Dayenu.

If women were in the Tribal Council and
decided on the laws
that dealt with women,
Dayenu.

If women had also been
the writers of Tanach,
interpreters of our past,
Dayenu.

If women had written the Haggadah
and brought our mothers forth,
Dayenu.

If every generation of women
together with every generation of men
would continue to go out of Egypt,
Dayenu, Dayenu.

LO DAYENU

If the Shekhinah had brought us forth
from bondage
and had not educated us,
it would not have sufficed us.

If She had educated us
and not given us opportunity to work,
it would not have sufficed us.
If She had given us opportunity to work
and not allowed us to advance,
 it would not have sufficed us.

If we were allowed to advance at work
but had to perform housewifely duties as
well,
Lo dayenu.

If we were aided by rabbinical decree
and treated with dignity,
Dayenu, Dayenu. It would suffice us.

"Did our mothers stay up all the night as we here learning stay the night?" asked the Wise Daughter.

SHE COULD NOT SLEEP THAT NIGHT

> When Sarah saw that she was barren and ill-regarded,
> she could not sleep the decades of nights.

> When Rebecca was taken from Aramea
> to the strange land of Isaac,
> she journeyed forth,
> and did not sleep those nights.

> When Leah was wed for only a week,
> then had to share Jacob with her sister
> Rachel, she turned her face into the pillow
> and did not sleep the night.

> When Yocheved and Miriam planned the rescue,
> they plaited reeds all the night,
> and could not sleep that night.

> When Ziporah the Midianite
> was left behind with her two sons
> while Moses went back into Egypt,
> she could not sleep the nights.

> When Miriam celebrated the Redemption,
> she gathered the women,
> and they danced and sang all the night.
> They could not sleep that night.

> When Miriam was cast low,
> she paced her tent in anger,
> and could not sleep the night.

When Deborah, the judge,
marched with the army to war,
she could not sleep the embattled nights.

When Yael, from the house of Ziporah,
murdered General Sisera, she had not
slept that night.

When Judith prayed from dusk to dawn
planning against Holofernes,
she did not sleep all that night.

When women plan their lives,
their battles and escapes,
they do not sleep the night.

We here gathered learning
on the Night of Vigil
will not easily sleep this night.

"I am tired of Miriam," says the Wicked Daughter.
"When will you find her?"

The One Who Does Not Know How to Question
looks at the mothers.

The mothers answer the unasked question:

FOLLOWING MIRIAM
We follow her cape,
through the cold night air.
We follow her wrapped figure
under the hot sun
to places unknown.
We entreat her to halt, to recognize us.
What is the way? we ask.
Her footsteps disappear
in the sand.
We find the map as we go along.

LIFT the fourth cup.
THIS IS THE FOURTH CUP OF WINE.
We drink the fourth cup of wine, saying, "I
have been in Egypt. I have been in the desert. I
have learned our history. And I am still on my
journey."

We have ended the Passover service according to its
order and new customs.

Under the wings of the Shekhinah, we fly homeward
to Zion in song.

"The Women's Seder is ended?" asks the Simple
Daughter.
"Soon," say the mothers. "Someone is waiting for us."
The Mothers and Daughters Open the Door and
Welcome the Prophet

> **Miriam Ha Nevia**
> **Miriam from the House of Levy**
> **Soon will come to us**
> **with timbrel and song**
> **Miriam, our prophet,**
> **will dance with us.**

Miriam enters for the Festival Meal.